THE WEBLOG HANDBOOK

THE WEBLOG HANDBOOK

Practical Advice on Creating
and Maintaining
Your Blog

REBECCA BLOOD

PERSEUS
PUBLISHING

Cataloging-in-Publication Data is available from the Library of Congress
ISBN 0-7382-0756-X

Perseus Publishing is a member of the Perseus Books Group.
Find us on the World Wide Web at http://www.perseuspublishing.com

Perseus Publishing books are available at special discounts for bulk purchases in the U.S. by corporations, institutions, and other organizations. For more information, please contact the Special Markets Department at the Perseus Books Group, 11 Cambridge Center, Cambridge, MA 02142, or call (800) 255-1514 or (617) 252-5298, or e-mail j.mccrary@perseusbooks.com.

Text design by Janice Tapia
Set in 11.25-point Dante MT by the Perseus Books Group

First printing, June 2002

2 3 4 5 6 7 8 9 10—04 03

To Jesse James Garrett

Contents

There is a new profession of trail blazers, those who find delight in the task of establishing useful trails through the enormous mass of the common record. The inheritance from the master becomes, not only his additions to the world's record, but for his disciples the entire scaffolding by which they were erected.

—VANNEVAR BUSH,
"AS WE MAY THINK," JULY 1945

Preface

Early in 1999, I discovered an intriguing kind of website. Maintained by individuals who were infectiously passionate about the Web, these sites consisted of endlessly updated pointers to other sites, usually accompanied by brash, even outrageous, commentary. In January of that year, one of these sites posted a list of twelve others, referring to them as "weblogs." Intrigued by their self-assured voices and the value I found in being referred to sites that were reliably smart, useful, and funny, I never looked back.

In April 1999 I began my own weblog, Rebecca's Pocket. Since then I have been privileged to watch a community form, define itself, grow, redefine itself, and grow some more. I have watched individual weblogs debut, mature, and die. I've seen the genre stretch to include a more diaristic style of site. I have read (and been interviewed for) mass-media pieces that seemed almost to get it, and many, many more that didn't have a clue. During this time, the community of webloggers has expanded far beyond anyone's expectation. New types and novel uses for weblogs surprise even the oldest, most visionary enthusiasts of the genre. The size of the weblog community now defies enumeration, and new weblogs are being created every day.

Webloggers are opinionated people, and this book is as opinionated as I am. It is a distillation of my best thinking about weblogs based on what I have observed, what I have done, and what I have learned. It is based on personal experience, but I have attempted to make it as fair and complete as I possibly could. Weblogs first rose to prominence as a means of personal expression. I have generally directed the book to the maintainer of the personal site, but I have addressed the issues of the business-oriented weblog when appropriate. Most of what I say will apply equally to everyone who maintains a weblog, whatever its purpose or type.

If you are interested in starting your own weblog, I hope this book will provide you with the inspiration and practical advice you need to do so. If you already maintain a weblog, I hope that *The Weblog Handbook* will provide you with new ways of looking at your weblog and the community of which you are a part.

Rebecca Blood
March 2002
www.rebeccablood.net

1

What Is a Weblog?

*A weblog is a coffeehouse conversation in text,
with references as required.*

REBECCA BLOOD

You may have seen them in your travels around the World
Wide Web. Some provide succinct descriptions of judiciously selected links. Some contain wide swaths of commentary dotted
sparingly with links to the news of the day. Others consist of an
endless stream of blurts about the writer's day; links, if they exist, are to other, similar, personal sites. Some are political. Some
are intellectual. Some are hilarious. Some are topic-driven.
Some are off-the-wall. Most are noncommercial and all are impassioned about their subjects. They are the weblogs.

What they have in common is a format: a webpage with new
entries placed at the top, updated frequently—sometimes several times a day. Often at the side of the page is a list of links
pointing to similar sites. Some sites consist only of a weblog.
Others include the weblog as part of a larger site. More than a
list of links and less than a full-blown zine, weblogs are hard to
describe but easy to recognize.

Personal sites and lists of links have existed since the Web
was born. Indeed, the ability to link from one document to any
other that existed on the global network was the great novelty
that drew early enthusiasts to the Web. Like a text version of
ham radio, early enthusiasts published pages and eagerly perused

the pages of others. It didn't matter what a page contained, just that it was accessible from any computer with a modem and a browser.

There has been spirited discussion in some quarters of the weblog community about when the first weblog appeared, but I think of Mosaic's What's New page, which ran from June 1993 to June 1996, as the progenitor of the format. Updated daily, it pointed Web surfers to sites they might enjoy seeing—and in those days Web surfers enjoyed looking at any page. Early adopters spent countless hours waiting for countless home pages featuring countless pictures of cats to download over their 1200 baud modems—and they liked it!

For a while, any webpage was an interesting addition to cyberspace, but then that space got crowded. Companies began advertising their products and services on the Web. More and more people put up pages about their lives and interests, and some of those interests were unimaginably arcane, esoteric, or just plain wacky. Newspapers and magazines published Web editions. The Web grew at an exponential rate and finding the "good stuff" became simultaneously more difficult and more time-consuming. But the good stuff was there, and enthusiasts enjoyed seeking it out.

And then an interesting thing happened. A few of these enthusiasts decided to put the links they collected daily onto a single webpage. Some of them had tired of spamming their friends with a constant barrage of email. Others had accumulated bookmark files that were bursting at the seams and sought a better way to organize the interesting things they found as they surfed. Whatever their reasons, for these folks it seemed the most natural thing in the world to put the record of their travels around the Web *on* the Web, and so a particular type of website was born. Enthusiastic surfers turned their home pages into a running list of links with descriptive text to inform their readers why they should click the link and wait for the page to download.

Steve Bogart created News, Pointers & Commentary (later called Now This) in February 1997, and Dave Winer launched Scripting News in April of that same year; Michael Sippey began The Obvious Filter (later Filtered for Purity) in May, and Jorn Barger's Robot Wisdom was created in December. And there were more, most of them completely unaware of the other sites that resembled theirs. Some called them "news sites" and some called them "filters," but most people didn't call them anything at all. "Links with commentary, with the new stuff on top" was the formula; for those who found them, these sites served as a welcome guide through the increasingly complex World Wide Web.

In November 1998 Jesse James Garrett, editor of Infosift, another of the original weblogs, collected a list of "sites like his" and sent them to Cameron Barrett, maintainer of Camworld. Adopting Jorn Barger's term "weblog" to describe the kind of site he maintained, Cam wrote an essay in January 1999 called "Anatomy of a Weblog," which detailed the elements of the form. He placed the list in a narrow column to the right of his weblog . . . and a movement was born. Maintainers of similar sites emailed their URLs for inclusion on Cam's list and readers suddenly had twelve, then twenty, then thirty and more weblogs to peruse in a day. No one liked the name very well, but with Cam's essay, "weblog" became the accepted term. Peter Merholz announced on his site that he was going to pronounce it "wee-blog" and it was only a matter of weeks before the abbreviation "blog" began appearing as an alternate term.

Most of the early weblog editors designed or maintained websites for a living. Even those who did not work directly on the Web knew HTML, the simple coding language used to create webpages. A few computer programmers designed systems to help them manage their sites, but most people updated their weblogs by hand.

Some Web designers created "arty" pages, but most weblogs were designed on the principle of simple functionality. A main area, wide enough for easy reading, was reserved for daily entries. Often a narrow side column echoed Cam's original list of "other weblogs" and this sidebar persists on many weblogs today. Jesse James Garrett added a link to his personal portal, a list of news sites, e-zines, and other weblogs. Partly convenience, partly an invitation to "see where I surf," in 2002 this convention persists even among webloggers who have never heard of Infosift.

Weblogs continued to spring up. Instead of being similar sites that had discovered a commonality, these weblogs were deliberately patterned after the weblogs listed on Camworld's sidebar. Many of them were created by Web developers who had coding skills and presumably spent their days in front of the computer. Unlike their coworkers, who sighed that the last thing they wanted to do when they got home was look at a computer, the webloggers were excited about the Web and passionate about its potential. They eagerly embraced the global network, looking first to the Web for news, information, and entertainment. It was natural that they would see their personal websites as extensions of their day-to-day lives.

Many of the first-wave weblogs updated throughout the day, providing a sort of real-time record of their maintainer's surfing patterns. They linked to general interest articles, to online games, and often to Web-related news. Camworld's sidebar continued to grow as these first-wave weblogs were added to his list of old-school sites.

One of these sites, Lemonyellow, was notable for being the first weblog to gain the attention of traditional media. The *New York Times* article about the site, published in July 1999, didn't say a word about weblogs, but it affirmed the notion that webloggers were on to something. Maintainer Heather Anne Halpert mixed links to interesting sites with esoteric entries about information architecture and notes on going to the theater. Her engaging style inspired open admiration. Literate, personal, and undeniably "thinky" in tone, Lemonyellow is, to my mind, the prototype of the notebook-style weblog. It ceased publication in April 2001.

In July 1999, Andrew Smales, maintainer of the popular weblog Be Nice to Bears, created Pitas, a service that enabled anyone with access to a computer with a Web browser to create a weblog entry by typing into a blank box and then clicking a button on the computer screen. A month later, a startup called Pyra produced a similar product called Blogger. With the introduction of these two services and the others that appeared quickly on their heels, anyone who could type and had access to the World Wide Web could create a weblog, and the bandwagon that had been steadily gaining momentum through the summer shot through the gate.

And weblogs changed. Weblogs devoted to short personal entries appeared, usually created with one of the simple new weblog tools. When these sites included links, if they did at all, they pointed mainly to other weblogs. In public and in private, webloggers engaged in vigorous discussions over the definition of the weblog. How often did it need to be updated? Every day? More than once a week? And most heatedly: Must it include links? In an attempt to organize the increasing mass of weblogs, weblogger Brigitte Eaton created a central weblog portal for the new community. Her criterion was simple: that a site consisted of dated entries. Since the Eatonweb portal was the most complete listing available, by default her inclusive definition won the day.

The weblog community spread to include sites that originated in Canada, Australia, the United Kingdom, and beyond. Numerous weblogs popped up in the Netherlands, which was known, for a while at least, as having the highest number of weblogs per capita in the world. Non-English weblogs proliferated, though they remained largely separate from the original community (Americans being, overall, relentlessly monolingual).

Today there are hundreds of thousands of weblogs, and dozens of software products designed specifically to make updating them easier. They have evolved to encompass any subject matter and they reflect worldviews that range from the private world of the writer to the public world of culture and current events, and everything in between. The appeal of each weblog is grounded thoroughly in the personality of its writer: his interests, his opinions, and his personal mix of links and commentary. These links point to anything and everything, from obscure articles about artists, to news analysis concerning current events, to the sites of his friends.

Each site is different—each writer decides each day what to write—but I place weblogs into three very broad categories: blogs, notebooks, and filters.

BLOGS: These sites resemble short-form journals. The writer's subject is his daily life, with links subordinate to the text. Even when entries point the reader to a news or magazine article, linktext gives the feeling of a quick, spontaneous remark, perhaps of the type found in an instant message to a friend. Links, when included, seem to be almost an afterthought, pointers to friends' sites or perhaps to the definition of a word. Completely unheard of when Cameron wrote his essay, this type of site dominated the weblog universe by the middle of 2000, probably due to the proliferation of tools that made posting a quick thought so easy that the addition of a link became seen as an unnecessary and (relatively) time-consuming step.

NOTEBOOKS: Sometimes personal, sometimes focused on the outside world, notebooks are distinguished from blogs by their longer pieces of focused content. Personal entries are sometimes in the form of a story. Some notebooks are designed as a space for public contemplation: Entries may contain links to primary material, but the weblogger's ruminations are front and center. Shorter than an essay, longer than the blog-style blurt, these sites are noted for writing that seems more edited than that of the typical blog. Both blogs and notebooks tend to focus on the weblogger's inner world or their reactions to the world around them; the links themselves play strictly a supporting role.

I suppose I should take a moment to differentiate both blogs and notebooks from online journals, which predate the weblog movement by many years. It is impossible to make a strict delineation; superficially, journals often contain one longer entry per day, one per page. Perhaps a deeper difference lies in the intent of the maintainer. Online journals are analogous to paper journals, with the sole difference that they are published for the world to see. Online journalers may keep a record of events, explore their inner world, or do any of the things that journalers traditionally have done with pen and paper.

Blogs tend to consist of much shorter entries, many per day, the blogger seemingly striving for communication more than self-enlightenment. Notebooks, while they sometimes use the "one entry per day" format, tend to be less a record of external events than a record of ideas, and those that focus on the personal tend to do so nonchronologically, dipping into their entire catalogue of experience to select individual stories rather than recount their journey day by day. In the end, it is the maintainer of the site who labels his work and chooses the community with whom he most closely identifies.

FILTERS: When I think of the classic weblog, I don't think of a short-form diary or a series of stories or short think pieces. I think of the old-style site organized squarely around the link, maintained by an inveterate Web surfer, personal information strictly optional. These weblogs have one thing in common:

the primacy of the link. Whether their editors write at length or not at all, filter editors want to show you around the Web. Some of these editors strive for pithiness, others for completeness, but even those who use links as a springboard to extended diatribes are focused primarily on the world outside their door. These sites may visually resemble the blog or the notebook, but they reveal the weblogger's personality from the outside in. The self, when it appears on a filter-style weblog, is revealed obliquely, through its relation to the larger world.

Some filter-style weblogs focus on a particular subject. The aim of these subject-specific filters is to provide their readers with a continuous source for all the available news about a given topic. Sometimes maintained by enthusiasts, sometimes by businesses or professionals, these sites are often designed to build and enhance the reputation of their maintainers.

Collaborative weblogs, as their name indicates, are maintained by a group of people instead of an individual. Usually filters, most collaborative weblogs are indistinguishable from an individually produced weblog, except that entries list several individuals as contributors. Some don't make even this distinction, and can be recognized only by reading the site's "About" page. Some collaborative weblogs are also community weblogs. These range from sites on which any member can post and comment, to those on which the site owners post to the main page and members contribute in discussion forums.

Of course, most weblogs do not strictly follow the roles I've outlined above. Blogs sometimes link to news articles or online games, notebooks sometimes contain one-line links, and filters sometimes contain linkless personal observations. It is just this variety in content and approach that makes weblogs so irresistible to many of us. Each weblogger creates a personal version of the weblog format, dictated by purpose, interest, and whim. The weblog is infinitely malleable and may be adapted to almost any end. There are travel weblogs, photo weblogs, sex weblogs, business weblogs, wedding weblogs, historical weblogs, humor weblogs, and weblogs focused on U.S. military actions. The very best weblogs, in my opinion, are designed to accommodate unexpected turns, to allow for a little experimentation.

◇ ◇ ◇

Weblogs Are Native to the Web

The weblog is many things to many people, but it is, above all, a form that is native to the Web. The traditional home page can range from an online resume to an elaborate family scrapbook, but it is generally an attempt to transfer the product of an older medium—paper—into the new. Intended to be updated infrequently, these documents create a fairly static representation of their creator. The weblog, updated regularly, is designed to be visited again and again, and most webloggers make a point of giving their readers something new to read every day. In other media, this takes the form of periodical publishing: editions put out at regular intervals. The Web enables continual publishing, in which updates can occur at any time; it is this aspect of the Web that weblogs can capitalize on. Whether or not the weblogger consciously associates the process of "updating" with the idea of "publishing an edition," the popularity of websites that track recently updated weblogs attests to this fundamental truth about the form.

The weblog points its visitors to other sites. Commercial websites spent years chanting the mantra of "stickiness": the ability to get visitors who came to their sites to stay there, even creating policies that prohibited the inclusion of external links anywhere on their sites. Weblogs have no such aspirations. Webloggers understand that people will regularly visit any website that reliably provides them with worthwhile content, even when that content is on another site. As counterintuitive as it may seem from an old-media perspective, weblogs attract regular readers precisely because they regularly point readers away.

The weblog phenomenon is democratic. Weblogs are generally published by a single person or a group of people who lack access to traditional means of broadcast. For this new type of publication, all that is required is reliable access to a computer with an Internet connection; free, easy-to-use services make it possible to produce a weblog without knowing HTML or spending a penny. In the weblog universe, everyone can say his piece. Produced without gatekeepers, weblogs focus on whatever topic is of interest to its maintainer: Web design, math-rock, world events, or day-to-day events. Webloggers who link to one another recognize their ability to leverage virtual social connections into ad hoc networks, enabling each of them to amplify his individual voice.

Weblog Filter Information

We are inundated with information; literacy and electricity have added to the din of the medieval marketplace an overlay of flyers, billboards, signage, and flashing lights. The unhappy combination of technology and hyperconsumerism has rendered our public spaces nearly uninhabitable. Radios blare out of car windows, bus stops promote shoes and sweaters, and long distance services advertise on coffee cup sleeves. Email, pagers, and instant messaging have accelerated the pace of personal communications. Televisions broadcast hundreds of channels and local newsstands carry thousands of magazines.

The Web, by allowing anyone on the network to access any and all information, has increased this din a thousandfold. Hobbyists and enthusiasts have created websites about every subject imaginable, including some that previously we had not imagined at all: The new information space includes a website devoted to the adoration of Converse's popular "Chuck Taylor

All-Star" sneaker, a site detailing the exploits of two friends who photograph each other attempting to match the appearance of strangers they happen to see, and one that seeks to elucidate an artist's curious obsession with young women holding celery. Additionally, online news outlets bring us up-to-the-minute details of important events and government sites provide the details of federal policy and congressional deliberations. With these new resources, just keeping up with the news can seem to be an infinitely expandable task; becoming and staying really informed has enlarged to become a full-time job. The terrible irony is that the more information is available, the less possible it is to know everything about even one subject. Because there is always more to know, it is increasingly difficult to feel that one knows even enough.

In such a world, the last thing anyone needs is another source of information. Indeed, for some people, this truly is the case. Some of us, having already hit our limit, have resorted to "news fasts" or to canceling all of our magazine subscriptions. Many of us return to our homes nightly unable to process any information that requires real thought or evaluation. Even for those who have not given up, interesting news goes unnoticed—and occasionally world events create so much news that no one can keep up.

Immediately after the September 11 attacks on the Pentagon and World Trade Center, the Web exploded. News outlets around the world pumped out story after story about the attacks and their ramifications: why they had happened, how they had happened, and what might happen next. Like everyone else, I was overwhelmed with the sheer amount of news and commentary that sought to make sense of the event, its aftermath, and its causes. For several weeks I found myself getting most of my news by reading other weblogs, whose maintainers seemed to have much more time than I had to comb through the available news sources. I used my weblog to cull from their sites the best stories they had found. I was, for a time, filtering the filters.

For everyone, the great task of the future will not be to gain access to more information, but to develop avenues to information that genuinely enhances our understanding, and to screen out the rest. For many people, weblogs provide this useful filter. Subject-specific weblogs link to the news they need in order to more effectively run their business or enjoy their hobby. Even general interest weblogs have great value for those too busy to do more than scan the headlines. When a reader shares a weblogger's general worldview, he can rely on her to point to articles and websites that will interest him.

Automated news aggregators, which collect the news on a given topic based on keywords, lack the human judgment to discern between two versions of the same story or to include a relevant story on a seemingly unrelated topic. Just as important, news selected by keyword is bound to leave a great deal of the world unheard of (and thus unconsidered) by the individual who relies on aggregators for his news. Even the man who turns first to the Sports section of the paper version of his hometown newspaper is exposed, however briefly, to the front news page; and an interesting headline in the Living section may catch his eye when he puts down the rest of the paper.

A good weblog on any subject provides a combination of relevance, intelligent juxtaposition, and serendipity. Read a good filter-style weblog for even a few days, and you will never doubt the value of an astute human editor. Because he evaluates content rather than keywords, a human editor provides his readers with more relevant information than the most sophisticated news aggregator ever can. Informed webloggers can add their own critical evaluation of the news they link, or link to someone else's opinion. More than anything else, the best weblogs create for their readers what I call "targeted serendipity." When a weblogger and his readers share a point of view, a weblog constantly points its readers to items they didn't know they wanted to see.

Weblogs Provide Context

One of the strengths of the weblog is its ability to contextualize information by juxtaposing complementary or oppositional documents and information. The Web allows easy access to numerous documents from a single source. When highlighting an interesting article, the weblogger can attach a primary source, a related news story, or a contrasting interpretation simply by adding a link.

Too often, mass media represent only the views of the powerful, ignore important context, or even misunderstand crucial facts. Individuals who recognize these omissions respond enthusiastically to small, noncommercial sites that aim to highlight easily overlooked stories or seek to put the news into a larger perspective.

Even the inclusion of an older news story can shed considerable light on current events, or just illustrate a shift in a newsmaker's public relations spin. Lawrence Lee of Tomalak's Realm has made an art of this type of contextualization. He regularly places older, related news stories alongside current articles on Web strategy. His unerring sense of the most relevant contextual material demonstrates the superiority of the human editor over news aggregators and computer-generated lists of articles sorted by keyword.

Webloggers unexpectedly turn out to be experts on all kinds of topics. All too often, corporate and political spokesmen skew the facts. When they are reporting on unfamiliar subjects or facing a tight deadline, reporters may accept this information at face value. Speaking from their own expertise or experience, weblog-gers frequently offer clear, cogent explanations of complicated topics. Even a weblogger who is not an expert may seek out additional material in an effort to discover whether questionable reported facts stand up to closer scrutiny.

Weblogs Promote Media Literacy

When a weblogger focuses on current events or pop culture, he is likely to begin reading numerous accounts of the items he links, looking for the best written or the most complete accounting. This activity alone is an education in media literacy. The inclusion or exclusion of a single fact can change the entire context of a reported incident and lead the reader to draw vastly different conclusions. The same facts, presented in a different order or described using different words, can convey vastly different messages.

After a December 2001 Supreme Court decision regarding the conviction of Mumia Abu-Jamal, I linked to the story on five prominent online news sites and reproduced their headlines on my site. These headlines described Abu-Jamal in wildly different terms, ranging from "cop killer" to "former radio journalist." The exercise was a stunning demonstration of the power of a headline—or even a short summary—to actively frame the facts and to prime the reader to draw a specific conclusion.

Composing linktext for any weblog, regardless of its subject matter, is an education for the weblogger. In summarizing an article, he must decide whether to employ neutral or value-laden language. He quickly learns that he has the ability, in his brief description, to draw the reader's attention to whichever aspect of the story he finds most compelling. Though he knows his audience will read and make their own evaluation, the weblogger will discover that he conveys his point of view in even the few words of his description. With each choice, the weblogger learns the power of a single word to affect the perception of his readers.

For the reader who follows several weblogs, the process can be equally instructive. When several versions of a popular story are linked by different weblogs, readers can easily evaluate each for themselves. And they will be unable to avoid noting the differences in tone and interpretation when different webloggers synopsize the same story.

Weblogs Provide Alternate Points of View

Weblogs are produced by every kind of person on any kind of topic. Because they are primarily noncommercial efforts, they have no vested interest in pleasing stockholders and no need to avoid offending advertisers.

Motivated webloggers seek out websites and articles from all corners of the Web. Marginalized voices, dissenting viewpoints, and obscure websites all flourish in the weblog universe. The Weblogger is free to link all of these things—and to comment freely—because he is beholden to no one. Since he makes no money from his site, he need never fear the loss of revenue from linking an unpopular article or stating an unmoderated opinion. The Weblogger may not be respectful or even nice about the sites and stories he links, but readers can be sure he is not speaking to placate an important advertiser.

Many of the newer webloggers are deeply committed to promoting their own worldview. They see their weblog as a personal op-ed column, a space in which they can proselytize their own way of thinking and pronounce judgment on the news and opinions of the day. These webloggers tend to link to opposing viewpoints only to attack them, and they can be counted on to provide a wide variety of links to other webloggers and columnists who share their point of view. Whether they inhabit the political left or right, these weblogs are reliable sources for a specifically slanted view of the world.

Other weblogs have a far less deliberate political bias. Though their sites reflect their maintainer's interests and general world-view, these webloggers may seek out unusual sources in an attempt to supplement the homogenous news that is spooned out by standard corporate purveyors. They may link to articles that go against the general political grain of their site, if they are interesting or likely to tweak their politically rigid readers. Whatever their motivations, weblogs that are maintained by information junkies are likely to bring to the attention of their readers websites and articles that would otherwise go unnoticed.

Weblogs Encourage Evaluation

The value of a weblog editor is not his objectivity but his predictability. By this I do not mean that webloggers should limit themselves to an approved set of topics, or that they should write only what they believe their readers have come to expect. Rather, readers who know a weblogger's biases can evaluate his writing with greater ease than they can an ostensibly objective news report. A weblogger's commentary may provide insight into current events and may provoke the reader to more fully consider his own point of view.

If a weblogger is inclined to be skeptical of mass media sources but accepts alternative sources at face value, his readers will quickly learn to account for that. If he is in the habit of linking to alternative sources in order to publicly discount them as nonsense, his readers will know what to expect. A corporate lawyer's weblog may provide his readers with analysis of intellectual property issues that they simply can't find elsewhere; knowing that he is deeply entrenched in the business world, they are able to evaluate his opinions on labor issues accordingly. Having learned an individual weblogger's predictable biases, readers know what to expect when they visit and can account for the assumptions that color both his choice of material and his commentary. Seeing this in the weblogs they read, readers may become more attuned to the biases that inform their other sources of information.

Webloggers naturally include links to the sites they recommend to their readers or to sites with which they agree. But when a weblogger links to a site in disagreement he invites the reader to evaluate both the link and the weblogger's opinion. In each case, the inclusion of that link profoundly changes the relationship between the writer and his readers, since the reader can easily access the primary material. The weblog audience is no longer forced to rely on the writer's synopsis of the source material—or on their own past reading; the hyperlink allows the weblog audience to read and evaluate for themselves the meaning of the source material cited. Based on that reading, it is a simple matter to decide whether the weblogger's commentary is insightful, obvious, or worthless.

Weblogs Invite Participation

With the addition of a comment system, many weblogs actively solicit ideas and opinions from their readers. Individual readers may offer alternate readings of linked articles, supplemental material, or additional views on the same topic. Even before the widespread adoption of comment systems, most weblogs provided an email address to the site's creator. When an article piques their interest, readers respond. My readers have recommended articles and resources for inclusion on my website, tried to demonstrate the error of my thinking, and offered thoughtful commentary on articles I have linked. They have sent me links to their own essays and thanked me for mine.

It is a long-standing tradition in the weblog community to actively solicit reader input and expertise. In response to direct requests, my readers have emailed me lists of San Francisco goth clubs, links to resources on world energy usage, and suggestions for a Subaru mechanic. At my request, they have recommended thoughtful right-wing publications and entertaining films.

Weblogs invite participation in another way—they produce webloggers. Reading the thoughts of others like themselves, ordinary individuals suddenly understand that on the Web anyone can speak their piece, and readers become writers.

Weblog as Method

It has become highly unfashionable these days to define the weblog in any way beyond its basic format. To do so is considered an affront to the creative impulse of thousands of personal publishing mavens. But I would argue that the weblog community has developed an approach that distinguishes the weblog from traditional media forms and gives it much of its strength. This approach is so ubiquitous that it is invisible to the community at large—except when it is violated. That approach is based on the link, because weblogs link to everything.

Is there an article a weblogger agrees with? He links to it. Is he acquainted with the maker of another personal site? He links it. Most importantly, is there an article, an essay, or a piece of commentary with which he disagrees? Did a politician make a speech he feels misrepresents the facts or betrays her basic immorality? If so, a weblogger will tell you exactly what he thinks about it, and he will accompany that commentary with a link to the piece in question so that you may simultaneously judge the words of his ideological opponent, and his evaluation itself.

The link is the fundamental attribute of the Web, and it is the single most important thing that distinguishes weblogging from traditional forms of publishing. I would go so far as to say that if you are not linking to your primary material when you refer to it—especially when in disagreement—no matter what the format or update frequency of your website, you are not keeping a weblog.

It is not required that all weblogs be centered on a list of links, only that every type of weblog, when referring to online sources, links to them.

It is the link that gives weblogs their credibility by creating a transparency that is impossible in any other medium. It is the link that creates the community in which weblogs exist. And it is the link that distinguishes the weblog—or any piece of online writing—from old-media writing that has merely been transplanted to the Web.

Weblogs and Journalism

While I consider weblogs a vital component of a healthy media diet, in the end, weblogs and journalism are simply different things. What weblogs do is impossible for traditional journalism to reproduce, and what journalism does is impractical to do with a weblog. To my mind, news reporting consists of interviewing eyewitnesses and experts, checking facts, writing an original representation of the subject, and editorial review: The reporter researches and writes a story, and his editor ensures that it meets her requirements. Each step is designed to produce a consistent product that is informed by the news agency's standards. Weblogs do none of these things.

Weblogs have no gatekeepers. They are generally produced in the maintainer's spare time. Webloggers do not employ fact checkers, and they answer to no one but themselves. Neither do webloggers generally produce their own articles about the events in their community, at least not the kind of articles that newspapers and magazines produce.

Occasionally, an accident of fate will place a weblogger in the midst of a momentous event: during the 2001 Seattle earthquake,

community members posted available information on the collaborative weblog MetaFilter, keeping each other and the rest of the
country informed until news organizations could catch up. Without question this is information sharing, but I think it is more
closely aligned with the emergency use of ham radio than with
traditional print and broadcast news.

Because the words are printed on a page, eyewitness accounts
may seem confusingly similar to newspaper articles. To be sure,
eyewitness accounts are the basis for many good news reports,
but these accounts can offer only one perspective of an event. A
good news story seeks to put eyewitness reports into some kind
of order, combining individual experiences to create a larger account, one that will tell a fuller story. The juxtaposition of many
eyewitness accounts is only that; it takes a skilled writer to com-
bine those accounts into a more complete narrative.

Similarly, the attacks on the World Trade Center were followed by an intense, compelling recounting of the incident and
its aftermath by dozens of webloggers who lived in New York
City. These stories are important narratives that provide personal, human detail about a situation that most of us could not
even have imagined. As with the Seattle earthquake, these were
eyewitness accounts, and they provided their readers with a level
of personal, emotional detail that is not supported by traditional
models of journalism. The enormity of the situation compelled
all who witnessed it to reassess their most deeply held beliefs;
especially for those who lived and worked in New York City, this
introspection was accompanied by gut-wrenching reflections on
right and wrong, and on the very meaning of life. These vivid,
personal stories transcend the bounds of news reporting; calling
them "journalism" does not convey their more enduring importance as narratives of a shattering human experience.

Weblogs can perform a valuable function as critical dissemi-
nators of pertinent information. Following the attacks, webloggers combed the media, reading and evaluating hundreds of

news accounts, op-ed pieces, and magazine articles. In a world that was suddenly awash with more information than anyone could hope to process, webloggers led the way. By reading and evaluating news sources from around the world, and scouring each other's sites, webloggers provided their readers with the most pertinent information available.

Webloggers come from all backgrounds and often provide their readers with highly informed explanation and analysis of news stories that are related to their fields of expertise. But an expert is not transformed into a journalist by the simple act of writing down his response to a current news story. Similarly, some webloggers provide their audiences with news from their industry, offering both an insider look at the latest events and informed pointers to news stories that are important from an industry perspective. All of this is valuable information, but news about an industry *from* that industry—no matter how factually accurate—is public relations, not journalism, which instead seeks to put every story in a larger context than any individual perspective can provide.

When you consider that news editors build their professional reputation as much on their ability to omit the unimportant as on their ability to judge what is worthwhile, I think you might make a case for the filter-style weblogger as news editor, and in fact many refer to themselves as the editors of their sites. When he takes the time to review numerous versions of the same news story, the weblogger is, in effect, deciding which reporter most compellingly makes her case. However, when you consider that the weblogger has no part in deciding what news will be reported, the case for the weblogger as news editor falls apart.

Collaborative sites like Slashdot, Kuro5hin, and MetaFilter are often cited as examples of peer-to-peer (P2P) journalism. On Slashdot and MetaFilter, editors or members post links and participate in discussions about the posted material. Kuro5hin goes even further: Members research and write original articles that other members discuss. At their best, discussions on these sites vastly clarify the linked articles by offering pointers to additional online material and expert information and analysis by qualified members.

Without question, these sites are fascinating examples of information sharing, analysis, and dissemination, and I believe that they may represent a genuinely new way for news to be collected, analyzed, and distributed. It is important to note, however, that the collaborative community structure of these sites is the key to this phenomenon; the weblog form has nothing to do with it. In fact, the weblog format may prevent these sites from investigating their subjects as thoroughly as they could: As material scrolls down and off the page, readers' attention is directed to other, more current matters. If these sites are examples of P2P journalism, it is because they bring many minds to bear on the news of the day; their format is, if anything, a hindrance to be overcome in order for the experiment to be carried to the next level.

I see certain weblogs as directly analogous to a form of traditional journalism: the opinion or analysis piece. For many webloggers, a weblog is above all an opportunity to pronounce their opinions on politics, world events, and the opinions of others. That they write three hundred words on six subjects every day rather than fifteen hundred words on one subject once a week is immaterial. These webloggers may not carry their ideas through as completely as the professional columnists they emulate, but their intent is the same—and I would argue that three hundred carefully selected words by a thoughtful amateur have more substance than fifteen hundred words of knee-jerk invective, no matter how much the professional has been paid. These webloggers see their weblogs less as filters and more as platforms for directed self-expression.

But none of this is unique to weblogs. Journalism's components—reporting, news analysis, news selection, and dissemination of information—have existed and thrived in other media long before the World Wide Web. Journalism begins with reporting; all of the other functions associated with the practice have been developed in support of this one essential objective. The weblog format is optimized for filtering and dissemination, but to make a case in those terms for weblogs as journalism is to confuse journalism with influence. One example will suffice: Oprah Winfrey has used her television show to educate her audience about many important issues, and a word from her can send a novel to the top of the bestseller list. Although she is an important media personality, I don't think anyone would describe her as a journalist.

Weblogs are not, as some people say, a new kind of journalism. Rather, they supplement traditional journalism by evaluating, augmenting, and above all filtering the information churned out by journalists and the rest of the media machine every day. Mass media seeks to appeal to a wide audience; weblogs excel at creating targeted serendipity for their individual constituencies. While they occasionally may even "scoop" traditional media by their proximity to noteworthy events, weblogs should not aspire to carve a place within the ranks of traditional journalism.

The weblog's strength is fundamentally tied to its position outside of mainstream media: observing, commenting, and honestly reacting to both current events and the media coverage they generate. Weblogs can function as superb digests of online material. They excel at exposing and explaining flaws in media coverage. There is no better source for finding lesser-known articles and obscure websites.

In the end, the weblog really is something new, something interesting and worthwhile in and of itself. It does not need to ride the coattails of journalism or, indeed, any older media practice to be worthy of respect and serious consideration. Both weblogs and journalism would do well to forget about defining weblogs as journalism, or expanding the definition of journalism to include the new form. Rather, each should recognize the strengths of the other and both should move forward to further perfect their own craft.

Referenced Weblogs

Now This	http://www.nowthis.com/log/
Scripting News	http://www.scripting.com/
Filtered for Purity (now defunct)	http://www.theobvious.com/
Robot Wisdom	http://www.robotwisdom.com/
Infosift	http://www.jjg.net/infosift/
Camworld	http://www.camworld.com/
Anatomy of a Weblog	http://www.camworld.com/journal/rants/99/01/26.html
Peterme	http://www.peterme.com/
Lemonyellow (Internet Archive)	http://web.archive.org/web/20000304010149/www.lemonyellow.com/archives/april99.htm
Be Nice to Bears	http://www.benicetobears.com
Tomalak's Realm	http://www.tomalak.org/
MetaFilter	http://www.metafilter.com/
Slashdot	http://slashdot.org/
Kuro5hin	http://www.kuro5hin.org/

Other Referenced Websites

As We May Think, Vannevar Bush	http://www.theatlantic.com/unbound/flashbks/computer/bushf.htm
Mosaic "What's New"	http://archive.ncsa.uiuc.edu/SDG/Software/Mosaic/Docs/whats-new.html
The New York Times profile of Heather Anne Halpert	http://www.nytimes.com/library/tech/99/07/circuits/articles/221emo.html
The Chucks Connection	http://chucksconnection.com/
Blending In	http://www.deanandnigel.co.uk/
The Peculiar Art of Mr. Frahm	http://www.lileks.com/institute/frahm/index.html
Pitas	http://www.pitas.com/
Blogger	http://www.blogger.com/
Eatonweb Portal	http://portal.eatonweb.com/

2

Why a Weblog?

Everybody is talented, original, and has something important to say.

Brenda Ueland

There are as many kinds of weblogs as there are kinds of people, but I suppose there are only three motivations for keeping one: information sharing, reputation building, and personal expression. Although any one of these may be the primary reason for a weblog, no one maintains a weblog for any length of time without eventually doing all three.

Whether you write about your avocation, your day, your business, or your take on foreign affairs, when you publish a weblog you are sharing information. As you research and write, you will gain expertise in your subject (even if that subject is nothing more than what catches your eye). As you publish, you will accumulate a body of work, no matter how short the individual entries, and in this you create an online representation of your thinking. Lest you think that only blogs and notebooks foster self-expression, consider that even a highly focused subject-specific filter with no personal commentary betrays, with the choice of its links, the sensibilities of its editor.

Weblogs Build Better Writers

It's easy to write poorly, but it's hard to write poorly every day. Wait. Let's go back a step: It's hard to write every day.

I don't believe I've read one book or interview on "being a writer" that didn't contain the same magical piece of advice: Write every day. But how hard is that? It's always been impossible for me. When I have a compelling idea or a pressing need, I write like the wind. At one job, I was known for writing lengthy, scathing letters to incompetent consultants and unscrupulous vendors. But writing every day? I wouldn't know what to say.

I created my weblog because I was finding so many interesting links, and I thought I had funny and occasionally insightful things to say about them. It was fun to surf the Web, and it was more fun to create a bit of linktext to frame the things I found. Once I started, I felt obligated to update my site on a regular basis. Usually this was easy, but on some nights I had trouble finding anything that seemed worthwhile, or I felt that I simply had nothing to say. But I had an audience, however small, and knowing that, I would dig a little harder or just keep trying until I had formed a coherent bit of linktext.

Perhaps it would be most accurate to say that when you are sincerely trying, it's hard to write poorly every day. It is possible to post weblog entries the way some people eat potato chips or change TV channels. These random bits of text will never be compelling. But if you have something to say, taking the time every day to write it down until it says exactly what you mean will make you a better writer.

After I started my site, I was surprised to discover that its very design improved my writing. I designed my site to accommodate smaller screens, and like many others, I included a sidebar, which further reduced the width of my main writing area. Forced to write in a small space, I used the fewest words that would express my meaning, and my writing became sharper, clearer, and more economical.

Writing short is hard—and very good for you. Seeking to distill your thoughts to the fewest words, you will find out what you really think, and you'll work even harder to find the precise term to express your meaning. Paradoxically, writing short also spurred me to write longer pieces. Finding that I sometimes had more to say than I could comfortably fit in a weblog entry, it was natural to turn my comments into an essay. Rather than distill my thoughts, this longer form required that I flesh out my ideas and more fully support my conclusions.

Composing linktext has given me practice in thinking through a subject by writing it down. Composing linktext and realizing the next day that it could have been better has taught me to critically, unmaliciously evaluate my own work. More importantly, it has given me practice in performing imperfectly in public and moving forward unashamed. Updating my site daily has taught me self-discipline and given me a reason to think deeply. I am a better writer.

Weblogs Build Self-Awareness

It is impossible to write down your thoughts every day without noticing what you are thinking.

A blogger who complains weekly that she is tired of her job will begin, eventually, to enumerate the particular circumstances that make her so miserable. Writing the same thing over and over, she will confront the problems she is not addressing and be moved to make a change. Looking back, she will find a record, however informal, of the progress of her life.

Notebooks work in a similar fashion, providing their maintainers with a place to simultaneously work out their thinking and track the course of their attention. And while it may seem that only blogs and notebooks promote self-awareness, the effect is just as pronounced for the weblogger who maintains a filter.

After producing Rebecca's Pocket for several months, I noticed how frequently I linked to articles on archaeology and scientific discoveries. I chose them because they seemed worth sharing, and in fact they were just the sort of stories I was apt to read aloud to friends when sharing a Sunday *New York Times* over a latte. But reading aloud is even more ephemeral than writing a weblog, and if you had asked me, I would have told you my major interests lay in the arts and humanities, and that I was only marginally interested in science of any kind. Indeed, I had completely forgotten that, for a short while as a child, I had dreamed of becoming an archaeologist. Reading the record of things I deemed worth sharing reminded me of a self that I had overlooked.

No matter how random or structured or impersonal a weblog may seem, each one, whatever its nature, provides for its readers an intimate portrait of its maintainer, a portrait drawn over time. Random observations, selected links, extended diatribes—accumulated, these elements resolve into a mosaic revealing a personality, a self. The effect is more profound for the weblogger herself. The weblogger is privy to the entries she posts and those that she does not: *I think I'll blog that!* followed a moment later by *No. . . .* Acutely aware of what she does not type, the weblogger more clearly defines her own boundaries. Reviewing what she has written, she catches glimpses of her less-conscious self.

Weblogs Build Critical Thinkers

The effort required to transform the feeling of "this is interesting" into a succinct description of why it is worth a read is the difference between knowing what you think and why you think it.

You cannot choose links for your website each day without practicing discrimination; every weblogger who maintains a filter quickly becomes aware that she is building her reputation with the links she provides, and as a result few people are willing to put just anything on their page. When a weblogger feels compelled to offer even a short comment to frame each link, she will have to decide what she thinks each article is about, or why she thinks it is worthwhile.

Webloggers committed to providing their readers with the best available links may find themselves reading and comparing two or three versions of a news story. Confronted with several versions of the same story, the weblogger will see how differently the same information may be framed and how the inclusion or exclusion of additional material can change the reader's impression of the facts. She may take the time to dig up additional material, either to support the linked article or to contradict it. Evaluating all these sources of information, the weblogger will be forced to judge the worth of each.

On the Web, information is easy to find. When a weblogger links to any source of information, she knows that her readers will make their own evaluation of the text. This is a considerable advantage to the writer who wishes to comment extensively on any document, since she can trust interested readers to have read the primary text. It may also keep her honest in her assessment of the material. If she misrepresents another writer's point of view, it will be instantly apparent to her readers, unless they are rabidly biased themselves.

Reading several webloggers' commentary on a single story, readers are bound to be surprised by the differing perspectives a single link can inspire. Webloggers often fundamentally disagree about various aspects of a current news story or event, but I think it's more interesting when three webloggers agree on the facts and interpretation but have entirely different views on why an event is important. Watching others elucidate their thoughts, the weblog reader considers her own interpretation.

Weblogs Build Reputations

Readers visit the sites they find to be interesting and useful. Weblogs can be both of these things. Even the individual whose weblog contains few links can, through her honesty, humor, and passion, build a devoted audience. Whether or not her audience is extensive, her words will create an online persona; and even if her weblog does not provide a tangible service, a blogger may become known as a fine writer or an entertaining storyteller.

Because they reflect individual interests, weblogs become resources for links and insight on specific topics. I may visit one weblog to see what the political right has to say, another for my daily portion of humorous news stories, and another to read the personal commentary of its maintainer.

Individuals whose weblogs focus on a particular topic become known as experts in their field. Providing a reliable resource for news about a certain topic is enough to gain you a dependable following among fellow professionals or aficionados. If you take the time to frame this information with your own remarks, you may be regarded as insightful and informed. If your subject matter tends to be particularly esoteric, you may gain a reputation as an intellectual. I have seen weblogs translate into employment, speaking engagements, and even book contracts.

Freelancers and small business owners can raise their profile by creating and maintaining a weblog that focuses on their field of expertise. Sharing information is one of the best ways to gain respect in any field. Once you would have had to publish a book or magazine article or speak at professional events, and these opportunities were rare unless you had already achieved a certain prominence. The Web has circumvented all the gate-keepers, and now everyone with a webpage has the means to reach an audience of like-minded individuals. A business wishing to build or leverage the existing reputations of its staff may want to publish a collaborative weblog in which each person contributes and comments on topical links.

If you hope to convert this prominence into actual revenue, focus on the needs of your customers. A plumber who maintains a weblog focused on the latest pipe fittings may acquire a devout audience of other plumbers, but this may not translate so readily into sinks to unclog. But if her weblog also includes information to help the homeowner troubleshoot minor plumbing snafus and to determine which are minor repairs and which should be attended to only by a professional, it may also help attract and keep loyal customers. Customers like to feel that they are dealing with trusted experts; your weblog can be your calling card.

Weblogs Build Connected Businesses

The business that can efficiently disseminate pertinent information internally will produce informed employees working toward the same goals.

Employees need help managing their time, and increasingly, managing time means managing information. No one needs more email streaming into their inbox. Companies that distribute information on changes in policy via email (or paper!) force employees to process, analyze, and file incoming notes, or risk losing valuable pointers to needed information.

A weblog is the perfect format for the top page of a company intranet. The weblog's reverse-chronological arrangement ensures that everyone visiting the page will see the newest information because it is always on top. Entries briefly summarizing each piece of content allow employees to judge whether the information is pertinent to them and whether they must respond in a timely fashion. More detailed information is always only a click away. Carefully constructed document titles and linktext ensure that local search engines will quickly locate relevant information when employees need it.

Distance becomes immaterial when employees have access to the same information at the same time: No one is ever left out of the loop. Because all important information is located on the Web, any employee with a network connection has access to the most current company information. Paper memos may be misplaced, but the Internet never gets lost; employees save time and space when company directives are filed for them on the Web.

The weblog format efficiently addresses many audiences at once. When I worked at a large university, I used our department intranet weblog to alert researchers to grant application deadlines and procedures; division administrators to resources relevant to managing their doctors' grants; secretaries to procedural changes in submitting complex paperwork; and all employees to information concerning their benefits packages and other department-wide concerns. In my experience, the more mired an organization is in arcane procedures and exacting paperwork, the more useful a weblog can be for communicating changes in policy and providing pointers to useful resources to help hapless employees navigate byzantine processes.

When information changes quickly or when staying abreast of industry developments is critical to a company's success, a weblog can provide the means for getting new, important information to every employee. Small businesses or working groups may create a collaborative weblog that will allow any employee to post relevant information or to organize supporting documentation. Groups may want to designate one employee to create a weblog highlighting any pertinent industry news. Such a weblog, designed to keep employees informed about their field, may serve a dual purpose as a reputation builder if opened to public view.

Who Should Weblog?

Like everything in life, a weblog will reward you in direct proportion to the effort you expend . . . up to a point. The happiness you derive from your weblog will depend on your interest, your ability to devote sufficient time to the project, and your commitment to keeping the rest of your life in balance.

Maintaining a weblog is time-consuming. I spend two or three hours a night on my weblog, surfing the Web, composing linktext, and perusing my server logs. Not everyone spends so much time. Some people, judging from their daily output, spend much more time than I do.

You are a good candidate for maintaining a weblog if you already spend hours online every day. If you sit down at the computer only to check your email and buy the occasional book, maintaining an online record of your Web travels or daily observations would probably constitute a dramatic disruption to your schedule. If, after spending your workday at the computer, the last thing you want to do when you get home is turn on your PC, you should probably take up knitting or join a film club instead.

If you spend little time on the computer but you need a good reason to write, a weblog may be feasible, but be aware that you will be replacing one of your current activities with this one. If you are interested in starting a weblog that focuses on your current hobby, plan to set aside a portion of the hobby time you already spend for maintaining your new site.

You can use a weblog to communicate efficiently with large or dispersed groups of people. I have seen them used to manage a college class, to serve as a private family journal, or to provide an ongoing record of a planned wedding.

If most of your Web time is work-related, and you think you have a good deal of knowledge to share with others in your field, consider asking your employer to sponsor an industry-specific weblog. I would begin by creating such a weblog in my spare time, spending evenings collecting links and adding them to my site. Do this for two weeks to see if you really want to as-sume this new responsibility, and to give yourself enough ma-terial to really demonstrate your proposal. It can be hard to explain the value of a weblog, but if you can show your boss several excellent examples of industry weblogs before unveiling your prototype creation, she may be willing to sponsor the site. Even if she is not interested, you may find that you love updat-ing your new site and choose to continue doing so as a hobby.

If you are comfortable sending email and enacting e-commerce transactions, you will be able to find a weblog management tool that you can understand and use. If you love to surf the Web and already—by design or by default—have time to do so, a weblog will be a natural evolution of your online time. If you are willing to devote some of your hobby time to connecting and informing other hobbyists, or if you believe a weblog will efficiently replace an activity you already spend time perform-ing, a weblog may be for you.

No matter what your situation, you have the greatest chance of enjoying and continuing your weblog if it is an extension of one of your existing activities. By folding your new pursuit into hours you already spend on another activity, your sched-ule will be minimally disrupted and you will not be forced to choose between doing two things. If keeping a weblog means adding one or two more hours of "schedule" to your day, I pre-dict that you will drop it in less than a month—the same rea-son many of us have difficulty maintaining an exercise program. But if, instead, a weblog is an extension of an activity you already enjoy, I think that you will find the time you spend to be very rewarding.

Business and Reputation Building Weblogs

Delaware Law Office	http://www.delawoffice.com/news.html
Librarian.net	http://www.librarian.net/
The Scoop	http://www.thescoop.org/
x-Blog	http://xplane.com/xblog/

3

Creating and Maintaining Your Weblog

Form ever follows function.
Louis Henri Sullivan

The only reliable way to determine whether you will enjoy maintaining a weblog is to try it. As with any new hobby, the trick with weblogs is to invest enough time to discover your level of interest, while spending as little money as you possibly can.

Your options range from using a Web-based service to create and update your weblog by typing entries and pressing a single button, to hand-coding your site: typing HTML into a text editor, creating your own graphics, and uploading it yourself to your own domain. Available software and services fit everywhere in this range, from the very simple to the more complex. Professional-level graphics software can be very costly, but most of the tools needed to create a weblog are free or available at very low cost.

Maintaining a weblog does not require the use of any particular tool or software. A weblog is defined by its format and method; the tools you use should be chosen strictly according to their usefulness to you. You belong to the community of webloggers if you create a page that is frequently updated with entries placed in reverse chronological order, with links to the online material you cite. Don't let anyone confuse you into thinking that specific software is required to do this. Weblogging is about personal expression, not about software.

Conversely, a site that uses a weblog-management tool is not automatically a weblog. I occasionally see a website that refers to itself as a "weblog," based only on the fact that certain software is used to update the site. Do not confuse the means of production with the product itself. And do not feel that in order to create a space for yourself on the Web you must maintain a weblog. Before there were weblogs there were online journals, e-zines (online independently produced magazines), photo albums, community bulletin boards, special interest resources, and home pages of all kinds. Choose the format that suits you best and use whatever tools that will allow you to maintain it.

Let me be clear about something else: I will not be recommending that you use any specific software or service. I am not in the business of building or promoting any type of weblog management software, and I do not use any of the available tools or services, though I have started experimental accounts with many of them in the course of researching this book. Nor do I have a vested interest in promoting any of the companies that produce these tools. Each software package has strengths and weaknesses. The tools I want you to use are the ones that allow you to most easily write and manage your entries.

Even if I had a favorite, software of this type comes and goes. What is available as I write these words may no longer be available when you read this page, and new, fabulous software may have been introduced in the intervening time. I can't predict. What I hope to do is to provide you with a general approach and the encouragement you need to try out the available offerings so that you can choose from among them.

Choosing Your Tools

In the beginning, weblogs were created by Web professionals or by hobbyists who had taught themselves HTML. If you are one of these people, you will find designing and maintaining a weblog to be a breeze. You already have the knowledge to evaluate and the skill to use any of the current weblog management tools. Even if you plan to code your site by hand, take the time to investigate the available tools; they can greatly simplify the management of your site. But these days most new webloggers do not have a technical background and for them there is a vast mysterious expanse between "I'm going to start a weblog" and "There! My first entry is up."

There is only one rule when selecting any tool or element for your website: Choose the one that most closely matches your needs. Since you are just starting out, your requirements should be clear: easy and free. (I have provided step-by-step instructions for setting up a practice weblog with one such service in Appendix I.) As you gain experience, you may want to invest in tools that are more sophisticated than the ones you will begin with. But if your weblogging experiment requires you to learn three complex software programs and a coding language or two, you'll never get out of the starting gate, or if you do it will be months from now.

Make no mistake; I encourage anyone who falls in love with weblogging to learn HTML and its many associated skills: The more you know, the higher your level of control (and thus self-expression). A bread machine will make bread, but the man who falls in love with baked goods will eventually want to make a croissant. To create the things he dreams of, he will need to learn about the properties of yeast and perhaps buy a baking sheet or two—though he may still rely on his trusty machine for his everyday loaf.

So, let's start at the very beginning. You will need a place to host your weblog and a way to update it. When you look at any website, your computer is looking at specially coded files that reside on a computer that is configured to publish webpages to the world. Your "host" will be one of these computers (sometimes called a server). From this computer your weblog will be viewable by anyone who knows the URL (Uniform Resource Locator), or what you may commonly refer to as the "Web address." Whichever term you use, it is the string of characters that you see in the top window of your Web browser, and it looks something like this: http://www.rebeccablood.net.

A few weblog management tools offer free hosting. Because all the details will be taken care of for you, one of these services is often the best choice for a beginning weblogger. These services have some drawbacks: Because they are free to anyone who signs up, the service may be slow and there may be outages (times when their hosting servers malfunction, preventing you from reading and/or updating your website). These services go through cycles as they become popular, their equipment becomes overloaded, they upgrade their machines, and then eventually become overloaded again. That said, to my knowledge these services all work very hard to provide good service for their users, and many webloggers have no desire to host their weblogs elsewhere.

All of these services have a link on the home page that will take you to a sign-up form. All of them require a user name and password, and maybe an email address. All of them will provide easy-to-follow directions for creating your new weblog. Spend a weekend or several weeknights signing up for a few of these services so that you can see what they offer and exactly how they work. Use Google to search for ["free weblog"] and [weblog "free hosting"] (omit the brackets and keep the quotation marks) to find the services that currently offer free weblog hosting.

Begin by making a list of the services you want to consider, and then go to each and create an account for evaluation purposes. You may be given a list of preferences to select from, or you may jump straight to the posting page. Some sites automatically create a list of recently updated weblogs. If you are given the option, make your test weblog private (which just means that your site will not be included on that list). For all intents and purposes, your site will be private until you publish the URL in a directory or give it to your friends. If you are very nervous about being discovered, title your test weblog with a fake name.

Play around a bit with the posting functions of each service and try out all or many of the available templates to see which one suits you the best. Try updating your new site. Don't plan on posting anything of importance, just start clicking links and pushing buttons to see what happens next.

Do this with several services until you find one that feels like a good fit. As you look at your weblog management page, ask yourself a few questions about the interface.

- Can you easily identify how to create and delete an entry?
- Can you easily change the way your site looks?
- How do you add the name of your weblog to the page?
- Does this service offer clear instructions?
- Is it easy to find help when you need it?
- Do you need to read the directions before you can actually use the service, or are many of the available functions easily understandable just by looking?
- Are there user forums where you can ask questions?

Put yourself front and center as you evaluate these products. It doesn't matter if the service looks well thought out and well documented if you have difficulty understanding what you should do next. It doesn't matter how many other people happily use the service or how many of them think it is simple to use. When you read the directions, do they make sense to you? Choose the service that you find easiest to use.

Once you believe you have made a decision, it's time for some serious play. Sit down and post whatever comes to mind. Don't worry, you can delete it later if you want.

"this is my first post."

"This is my second post."

"I am a weblog stud."

"what does this button do?"

Of course, they will appear on your weblog like this:

what does this button do?
posted by rcb 12 December 2001, 2:20pm

I am a weblog stud.
posted by rcb 12 December 2001, 2:18pm

This is my second post.
posted by rcb 12 December 2001, 2:14pm

this is my first post.
posted by rcb 12 December 2001, 2:13pm

That's the convention: last post on top, and all front page posts in reverse chronological order. It's just an intelligent way to structure a webpage that will be updated frequently, since your browser automatically starts at the top of each page it visits. No one wants to scroll down to the bottom of the page (or even the current day's section) to see if any new content has been posted. With new content at the top, a visitor can see at a glance whether your page has been updated and easily begin reading your latest entries without any additional effort. A few webloggers prefer to create a new page each day they add content, but weblogs will most commonly feature several days' content on the front page.

Goof around with your weblog management service until you are very comfortable posting entries. By now you have identified one or two front-runners in your quest for the perfect starter service, so spend some time determining how easy it will be to customize the look of your page. Look at the available site design templates and begin to think about the specific elements you want to include on your weblog.

Conventions

Weblogs have been recognized as a form only since 1998, but in that short time a few conventions have emerged. Obviously you need not adhere to all of them (or to any of them), but I think it is good to know what they are, where they come from, and why they exist.

ARCHIVES: Most webloggers archive their entries. Any weblog management tool will do this for you automatically, and this alone is a good reason for even a skilled Web designer to consider using one of these services. Archives are handy when you want to reference a previous entry, they allow other webloggers to reference your entries, and they are fun to look over after you've been keeping a weblog for a while. The kinds of things I wrote about when I began my weblog and the ways in which I wrote about them are very different from my current style. In my archives I also maintain old site designs, so it's really like traveling back in time when I look at an entry from 1999. I enjoy observing the ways in which my site has changed and the ways in which it is the same.

If your weblog contains many links, you will find that many of them have a very short life. News articles are removed from news sites, URLs to former e-commerce sites are redirected to porn sites, and personal pages just go away. Some webloggers (a very few, I judge) go through their archives weeding out these bad links; others find that maintaining their current weblog is a full-time job and leave old entries intact as a sort of historical record. Neither approach is wrong, and you can use special software to alert you to dead links if at some future time you decide that you would like to bring your archives up to date.

One school of thought regards the weblog as something of a performance piece, resolutely refusing to archive entries for more than a month, if at all. It's up to you. I find my archives to be invaluable as a crude storage system. In composing daily entries, I have more than once referred to a previous entry; sometimes I just get a hankering to see something delightful that I featured in the past. If you choose to go the Way of No Archives, you need not apologize for it to anyone, but be sure that your decision is well grounded in a strong personal weblogging philosophy so that you will not have regrets if you find yourself longing for an old link or entry. Most weblog management software will allow you to switch your archives on and off, in case you change your approach.

Copyright Notice: You may want to add a copyright notice to the bottom of your page. If you are using a template designed by someone else, your copyright would extend only to your own writing, photographs, and other original material. You should know that all work you create is automatically copyrighted when you create it, whether or not you add such a notice to your site. I don't think anyone is going to steal one of your entries in its entirety, but photographs may be stolen. As unlikely as it is that an individual who is inclined to steal another's work will be stopped by a simple copyright notice, it is never a bad idea to remind them that your original work is protected. And it may be that a copyright notice adds a bit of legitimacy to your page. Not for anyone else. For you. Some of us never take our talents quite seriously enough, and a little subliminal message to remind us that our work has value is never a bad thing.

If you are creating a corporate weblog, you will want to place a copyright notice and notice of trademark on your site. It may be wise for you to include a privacy policy on your corporate weblog as well. Your lawyer and good judgment will tell you what, if anything, you need to protect on your company's website. If you participate in a collaborative weblog, decide whether the copyright of each entry belongs to the individual who posts it or to the weblog (organization) itself. Your contributors should understand who owns the rights to their entries before they post.

EMAIL ADDRESS: Most webloggers provide their email address somewhere on their site as a matter of course. Not only does this allow your readers to contact you to share their thoughts on your commentary, it allows them to let you know if something is wrong with your site. Other webloggers, in particular, are fantastic editors, and I have often been alerted to a misspelling, broken link, or HTML snafu by one of my generous colleagues. Additionally, readers (and even other webloggers) will sometimes send you links to articles they think you might want to consider publishing. Webloggers ask questions, readers send answers; webloggers make uninformed statements, readers send additional facts for their consideration. The email address makes it all possible.

SIDEBAR: Though some people choose to create an entire portal page, the sidebar is a time-honored weblog tradition, stretching back to Camworld's original collection of weblog links. Depending on the number of sites you regularly read (and your font size) a sidebar may contain plenty of room for you to create a miniportal that links to your favorite news sites, work-related sites, and of course a list of your favorite weblogs. It's a real convenience to go to a page—your own website—and have there a list of every site you regularly visit.

I've always felt there was another more subtle purpose to the sidebar. When Jesse James Garrett collected that original list of "sites like mine" and Cameron Barrett placed it in a narrow column to the right of his weblog, they both meant that the format and purpose of those sites was very similar to their own. This original list made no distinction based on the weblogger's writing style or subject matter; that it was a weblog was distinction enough. I believe that new webloggers are applying nearly the same criterion, only now "sites like mine" refers not to the format of the linked site, but to its spirit. Listing the sites he loves, a weblogger is aligning himself with his tribe.

When I look at an unfamiliar weblog, I always take note of the names listed in the sidebar. The first question I ask (still) is "Am I listed?" Pathetic, isn't it? I don't think you ever outgrow it. The second thing I ask is "Who is listed?" and at a glance I can provisionally (and usually pretty accurately) peg its creator as a "thinklogger" or a "progressive" or a "design kid" or one of any number of Web clusters that are defined by their similar approach to the world. It's natural to be drawn both to those who share your values and to those who embody your aspirations. Linking to the weblogs you admire can be a convenience to you, a service to your readers, and an introduction of sorts to the writer on the other end of the link.

On occasion I have seen the sidebar used as a miniweblog. Many others use their sidebar to create a personal snapshot, listing their current reading, music rotation, recent films, videos, and the like.

PERMALINKS: Pioneered by Blogger to accommodate the casual, conversational style of the typical blog, a permalink allows other weblogs to link to anything you post.

Because weblogs are updated frequently, entries are regularly deleted at the bottom in order to keep the front page at a reasonable size. This creates a problem for anyone wishing to reference a weblog entry on another site. Not only is it awkward to link to another weblog with a note to "scroll down to the January 26 entry," it's impractical. That entry will only be there for a limited time.

A permalink is a link before or after each weblog entry that takes the reader to its home in the archives—the permanent link. This allows other weblogs to create a reliable link to any post on your weblog. Once you start using them, you will be surprised at how useful they are even to you. I frequently find myself linking back to an earlier observation in order to contextualize a current entry.

SEARCH: Not only is it a real convenience to be able to search your own weblog for entries on past subjects, a search engine on your site is a kindness to the people brought there by a general Web search engine. As you accumulate archives, you will be catalogued by search engines for more and more phrases and terms. A Google search for "acquired situational narcissism," "barefoot architect," or "necked girls" will bring you to Rebecca's Pocket. But unless the search engine points you straight to an archive page, you could never hope to find the corresponding entries by just poking around. Several free search engines are available for your use. See which services other weblogs use or search Google for ["free search engine"]. You will need to be willing to learn a little HTML to fully customize most of them, but they generally provide clear, easy-to-understand directions to get you started.

COMMENT SYSTEMS: Rarely encountered only a few years back, the ability for readers to comment on individual weblog posts is increasingly common. Some of the more advanced weblog management software automatically includes this capability, but most of the simpler services do not, though add-on software is available. There are two things you must know about adding comment functionality to your site. First, discussion forums require management. Some people are very skilled at initiating and directing interesting online conversations; for others this is a chore. It's possible that no one will post comments to your site—or your readers may engage in heated arguments. You will want to check in at least once a day, likely more often, to respond to reader input and to ensure that all participants are behaving themselves. If you don't have time to manage active discussions, or if you will become depressed if no one comments on your posts, leave the functionality off.

Second, some of the available comment software can really slow down your site. Pages that should take just a few seconds to load take much longer instead. Read the documentation to see if there are any known issues. Note what comment software other webloggers use, and ask them about their experience. If your site takes a long time to load, readers will go elsewhere. Not only will your discussion forums remain empty, your weblog itself will go unread.

Design

Most, if not all, weblog management services will offer you a variety of site design templates to choose from. Once you figure out how to use a service, take some time to look through their templates and try a few on your practice site to see how entries look when surrounded by different designs. I think it is important that you like looking at your own site.

These publicly available templates have been created or chosen by your service for their suitability for weblogs, and you will find that many of them are similar. The very simplest weblog design consists of a header containing the name of the site with entries below. Often there is a sidebar or even two, one on each side of the main content area. This is the classic weblog design, and the vast majority of weblogs employ some variation on this theme. A look at a dozen weblogs will show you how different these variations can be.

When you are choosing a template or designing your website, go back to the primary rule: Choose the tool or element that most closely matches your needs. If you intend to post photos to your weblog, make sure your content area will accommodate a reasonably sized image. If you believe you will be writing long posts, write one or two (even if they consist of nonsense) to see how the text will flow in the available space. If the area is so narrow that your readers have to scroll down and down to read through a long sentence, another template may be more suited to your purposes. On the other hand, if your posts are likely to be quite short, perhaps a more narrow content area will be more pleasing to your eye. Is the text too small? If it is, is there an easy way for you to make it bigger? If your weblog is intended to keep your grandmother updated on your daily life, it will be important that she can read it.

Many of the free weblog hosting services have set up community forums that allow you to ask questions about the software. The software creators and other users are usually very generous with their knowledge. If your only complaint about an available template is the font size or the background color, use these forums to ask, first of all, if you are permitted to change these elements, and second, if it can be done easily, and if so, how. If you are not familiar with HTML, and your complaint is with the design of the template (for example, the width of the sidebar or size of the main content area) choose another template rather than try to make these structural changes.

It may be that you are allowed to change minor design elements and that a fellow weblogger teaches you how to make the background of your weblog blue. It may be that the ease with which you can do this tempts you to try other changes on your own. Take my advice and start a new weblog, a private one that you can use to experiment with HTML and its associated disciplines. Once you begin posting in earnest, you do not want to risk rendering your public weblog completely unreadable through the application of some color or other effect that you do not remember how to undo. I would encourage you, if you have the interest, to use your existing template (always in a private, separate weblog) to learn more about HTML. One way to do that is to look at the source code of other sites and learn how it works by playing with the elements to see what happens. This is a fine learning exercise, but always remember that making a few minor changes to a design does not make it your own. When you decide to unveil an original webpage design, make sure that it is one you created from scratch.

It is illegal to copy someone else's Web design and use it on your own site, just as it is illegal for anyone to change a few words in one of your posts and pass it off as their own work. Those who "borrow" other people's designs are usually discovered by a third party who quickly informs the real designer. It is easy for anyone who knows a little HTML to compare the code of two sites and tell if one was copied from the other. Web design pirates are universally despised by the Web design community, and so many webloggers are designers (even if they only design sites for themselves) that it is foolish to risk the ill will of so many.

If you want to use a variation on someone else's design, you must ask permission to do so. Be prepared to be declined; most designers have worked hard to create a look that is unique and few will be prepared to share it. If you do find a generous soul who is willing to let you do so, always credit them. A simple notice saying "Design based on example.com; used with permission" will defuse the animosity to which you will otherwise be subjected. Be sure that example.com links back to the original so that there can be no suspicion of deception.

If your style of posting changes drastically, you may become dissatisfied with your current design. You may be posting one lengthy entry a day; or your entries may have become shorter and pithier. Perhaps nothing significant has changed, but you find yourself a bit bored with the same old look. Whatever your reason, it is your space. A few of your longtime readers may miss the old look, but they will adjust, and your enthusiasm for your site will be renewed.

If you are already skilled in designing and coding websites, your weblog will provide you with an opportunity to create fun, non-commercial designs and perhaps to augment your coding skills. Some webloggers are relentless redesigners, and if this makes you happy, why not? For you, design is a way to express yourself, and your design is as much a means of communicating with your audience as are your words.

Apart from usability issues, I rarely see discussions of the effect that Web design can have on the viewer. I was puzzled for months about the popularity of a site that had the most garish background I have ever seen. I would go to the site, read an entry or two, shrug my shoulders, and leave. I visited this site whenever another weblogger pointed me that way, and again and again I was perplexed with its popularity. One day I clicked through to find a much less cluttered design. I read an entry—it was hilarious! I read another. It was equally funny. I began visiting the site regularly and I was amazed to discover that its author's delightful sense of humor had been completely obscured for me by his old design.

I favor clean, uncluttered design, and I would argue that on a weblog every element should be carefully designed to frame the content rather than compete with it. But that's my aesthetic. You may find my site boring and wish for something "more dynamic" or "cozier." If your website is a personal project, choose a design that pleases you and consult with no one else. Those who share your aesthetic will be drawn to your site.

Naming Your Weblog

You may already have a name in mind, or you may still be thinking about it. The only hard and fast rule is to select a name that is unique to your weblog; you don't want your site to become confused with an existing weblog. If you are having difficulty, think of the kinds of things you plan to write and see if that suggests a name. Make a list of the qualities you would like your weblog to embody; if that doesn't give you a potential title, get out a thesaurus and look those words up to see if any of the synonyms do. Take out that old list of potential rock band names and see if any one of them would suit your blog. Write down a few names and say them out loud. At some point you'll discover one that will just sound right. To make sure that the name you have selected isn't in use by another weblog, search Google and Daypop to see if anything comes up. If the first name you selected is already in use, rinse and repeat until you find one that will be unique to your weblog.

Going Public

You have determined which free weblog service is easiest for you to use; you have carefully read their terms of service so that you know exactly what you may and may not do; you have selected a design for your weblog and chosen your preferences; you have given your weblog a name and deleted all of your test entries. It's time for you to make your first weblog entry. Do you have anything to write?

I would like to suggest that you give yourself anywhere from a week to a month of regular updating before you publicly launch your new weblog. At the very least this will give your readers a small selection of entries to read when they first visit your site, but more importantly, it will give you the time to get into the flow of posting regularly and to begin to identify your personal style.

What will you write about? The answers may surprise you a little. You might imagine that you will focus on political commentary and find that you can't resist posting the wackiest links and articles that you can find. You may plan to write long, meandering musings about the meaning of life and discover that what pleases you most is to post short, cryptic comments about the people you work with. Take the time to discover the shape of your weblog by writing it, not by forcing yourself into a predetermined mold. It may be that you have much wider interests than you had realized; what you had envisioned as an antique dolls weblog may fit you better as a general interest weblog with frequent news about dolls. Or, beginning with the intent of writing about whatever comes to mind, you may discover that you enjoy writing most about a small, focused set of topics. Your weblog may look very much like the one you imagined, or it may be a complete surprise every day you put it together. Give yourself time to find out.

If you include links to other sites in your weblog, be sure not to click any of them until you are ready for other webloggers to find yours. When you click through to another site, it will automatically record the URL of your site as a "referring website." If you are linking to a major news site, it's unlikely that anyone will notice your URL, but if you link to another weblog chances are that its maintainer will click through to see who has linked to them. I was astonished one week after beginning my weblog to find an article "via Rebecca's Pocket" on one of my regular reads. I was flattered and a little dismayed; I remember thinking, *Oh, crud! Now I need to keep doing this!* If you want to have a private tryout period, admire your sidebar but do not use it.

Once you have produced your weblog for a week or two, spend an evening thinking about your comfort level and your audience. Ask yourself whether you are anxious to burst upon the weblog scene, or if the thought of writing in public makes you very nervous. Consider the possibility of your weblog being read by your family and friends, or by those webloggers who inspired you to create a weblog in the first place. Pay close attention to the way you feel when you imagine each of these groups reading your site.

Some webloggers make a point not to mention their sites to their parents simply because they want the freedom to say their piece without having to edit themselves for parental approval. I know of one weblogger who told no one he knew about his site. His audience developed when the sites he linked found him and linked back. Unless you use a fictitious name or no name at all, chances are good that at least a few of your friends and family will find your site eventually, but if you feel intensely uncomfortable at the thought of performing in front of your friends, by all means don't tell them. If it is easier for you to express yourself publicly to strangers, allow yourself the privacy to begin your new project unimpeded by the imagined presence of anyone you know. If you are very comfortable writing for your friends but terrified of what anyone else might think, send your acquaintances the link to your weblog when you are ready, but don't publicize it further.

I can guarantee that if you write every day, you will gain more confidence in your own point of view. I predict that after a few months, the thought of being read by your most dreaded audience, whether that be family or strangers, will no longer be cause for alarm. If it still is, continue as you have been, making your URL available only to those audiences with whom you are comfortable. I will remind you again that your weblog is intended to benefit you, and I want you to take that thought to heart. The best way for you to maintain your weblog is the way that gives you the most pleasure. If you do not honor your own limits, you will not enjoy maintaining your site. What is the point of designing your new hobby so that it is guaranteed to be no fun? If you are maintaining a personal site, you are obligated to no one. Write for yourself, and show it to whomever you please.

Once you have written long enough to have established a schedule, an approach, and a strong sense of your intended audience, it's time to go public. If you want to write for the world, switch your preferences from "private" to "public." If you are comfortable writing for your family and acquaintances, email them the URL. If you are producing your weblog for a small, private audience, send them the URL and ask them not to pass it on to others.

Whether your intended audience is large or small, public or private, you now have some extra motivation for writing as frequently and as well as you can. Knowing that someone is reading your site, you will unconsciously seek to express yourself a little more clearly and will likely be anxious to maintain a fairly steady publication schedule. Whatever your purpose and area of interest, you have a forum in which to speak your piece. Congratulations! You are now a weblogger.

Referenced Websites

Google	http://www.google.com/

Find a Weblog Management Tool

Google directory of weblog tools	http://directory.google.com/Top/ Computers/Internet/On_the_ Web/Web_Logs/Tools/
Weblog Madness Roll Your Own	http://www.larkfarm.com/ wlm/roll_your_own.htm

4

Finding Your Voice

*No one can be exactly like me. Sometimes even
I have trouble doing it.*

TALLULAH BANKHEAD

What makes great weblogs great? Some cover their chosen
topic with such thoroughness that they become the authoritative source for information in their field. But even these
weblogs can't cover every single bit of information that may appear in a week, especially since most are single-handedly produced by individuals in their spare time. Besides, a weblog that
thoroughly aggregated all the information on a topic would be
only that, a news feed; a weblog is the result of human selection
and reflection.

The elements of a superior weblog are identical for the blog,
the notebook, and the filter: point of view, discrimination in
choosing links, and the life experience of the writer. It is the
writer's unique fusion of interests, enthusiasms, and preju-
dices—her personality—that makes a weblog compelling. In
short, a weblog's quality is ultimately based on the authenticity
of its voice.

Personal detail is not necessary for "voice," but every good
weblog has a point of view, whether it is openly articulated or
whether it is made evident through the material the weblogger
chooses to link. Wood S Lot is a fine example of the importance

of the human editor, and the ability to build a reputation based strictly on the merits of the material one links. Its editor, Mark Woods, has done a remarkable job of providing a daily compendium of links about art, philosophy, progressive politics, and literary culture. He works almost exclusively with headlines and pull quotes, and while you'll rarely hear Mark speak directly, his voice is strong.

Defining Your Purpose

It is not important that you know exactly what you are doing when you begin writing your weblog, but you must have at least a loosely defined purpose for your site, and you must vaguely know for whom you are writing—or perhaps more importantly, for whom you are not. This will prevent you from making a few critical misjudgments, and from there your weblog will begin to take on a shape of its own.

But let's start at the beginning.

What is the purpose of your weblog? It can be anything: keeping in touch with friends and family, promoting your business, seeking to influence opinion, or even providing emotional therapy. I would define four broad purposes for maintaining a weblog, though most weblogs serve more than one of them: self-expression, keeping in touch, information sharing, and reputation building.

SELF-EXPRESSION: Some people simply want a space to write. For them, a blog can be a place to vent, to observe, to gloat, or to be silly. Ranging in form from numerous short bursts of thought to one longer, more focused piece a day, these weblogs are a personal creative space. For Web designers, a weblog can be a place to really play with the medium, frequently redesigning in styles that no commercial client would consider. Some people have created photo weblogs or weblogs made entirely of other kinds of images. Others use current events and links to other sites as a springboard for their own essays.

Every weblog, no matter what its purpose, will deepen its maintainer's creativity. Having to produce something for your weblog several times a week will force you—or give you an excuse—to practice your craft, whether it is writing or pulling out your camera to take a few shots. A weblog will invite you to expand your range by requiring you to write explanatory text even if you are "not a writer," enticing you to post photographs even if you are "not an artist," and inspiring you to write a full-length essay when you find yourself running out of space to fully express your opinion in your weblog proper.

Writing short is hard, and the daily practice of having to summarize or analyze an article with concision will make you a clearer writer and a better thinker. Even the practice of contextualizing an article with links to related (or tangential) material will exercise your creativity, encouraging you to make connections you might not have made otherwise. Many webloggers are motivated to learn more about Web design or to expand their coding skills in order to add functionality to their site; because their reward is a better weblog, this becomes a fun project instead of a tedious task.

And something else: Because you know how hard you are working, because you can feel yourself stretching each time you try something new or a little risky, maintaining a weblog will give you a new confidence in your own creativity, especially if you have habitually thought of yourself as an "uncreative type." It is hard to give credence to the idea that you have nothing to say when you are posting every day; and the notion that you are not creative becomes laughable once you regularly begin exploring new ways of expressing yourself.

KEEPING IN TOUCH: For many people, a blog-style weblog is an efficient way to keep in touch with family and friends who, for whatever reason, they seldom see. This may take the form of a weekly update or an endless stream of minutiae that, added together, create a detailed portrait of their lives. By frequently posting the news of the day, these webloggers create an online answer to the ritual "How was your day?" and keep their loved ones informed about the meaningful and inconsequential events of their lives. Most webloggers have found that even a weblog that was never intended to convey personal information will, when not updated for several days, generate a note from their mother asking if they are feeling well.

INFORMATION SHARING: Weblogs may be designed as a resource about a particular topic, or they may link to whatever strikes their editor's fancy. In the very early days, the weblog was compared to the "Wunderkammer," a traditional German cabinet of curios, and some weblogs still fit that description. But even in those days, no one definition adequately described the range of subject matter covered by the various weblogs; today such a comprehensive definition would be even harder. Some weblogs are focused on current events, some on funny links; some are general interest, others are focused on a single topic. Some webloggers strive to introduce their readers to only the weirdest, most obscure webpages, others to provide a running commentary on the news.

Those who maintain this type of weblog are typically news junkies, inveterate Web surfers, or expert Web searchers. They spend a lot of time on the Web and they love to share their finds with others. They share what interests them most, and you can learn a lot about even the most private weblogger by paying attention to her subject matter and commentary. Some editors log items so that they can find them again. If this is your purpose, you will want to install a search engine on your site and take particular care in composing your linktext so that a search for an obvious term will bring up the appropriate results. It is extremely frustrating to have to read three full months of entries to locate a link you distinctly remember logging, but can't locate with your search engine.

REPUTATION BUILDING: From the start, certain individuals and even businesses recognized that maintaining a weblog in their area of expertise would allow them to keep up with and organize information pertaining to their field while developing a Web-wide reputation as experts in their chosen profession. The first of these individuals were Web designers, but this strategy could be used by anyone, even hobbyists, whose colleagues research their field using the Web. These weblogs use every form and combination of links and text, from occasional links interspersed with lots of commentary to carefully selected links with little or no commentary at all.

In every case, readers come first for the information the site provides, but as time passes, the weblog editor, by association, acquires a reputation and soon her commentary takes on an importance it did not have only months before. It's less bogus than it sounds. By maintaining a weblog that is tightly focused on a particular subject, these weblog editors educate themselves by searching the Web daily for news and information pertaining to their area of expertise, exercising judgment in weighing the relevance or importance of what they find, and articulating their thoughts on the links they decide to include, either by summarizing the article or by analyzing the material presented. It is what experts do, and this practice will speed anyone's progress to that end.

Make no mistake, this works. I've seen businesses and especially individuals make names for themselves, going from unknown to "expert" in a year by providing a hub of information about a specific profession. When a reader's first impulse upon wanting information about a given subject is to visit a topic-driven weblog, it is a small leap to hire its editor to speak, consult, or otherwise practice their craft when the need arises.

Some reputation-building weblogs are maintained as part of a larger company site, which naturally includes the organization's contact information; reputation-building weblogs that are maintained by individuals, especially freelancers, often include a link to their resumes and may announce their attendance at conferences (especially when they are speaking) and other professional events. It is natural for any weblog to change over time to reflect the interests and purposes of its editor, and readers of established weblogs are often willing to pick through some detritus for a reliable ration of pertinent information; but even one of these long-standing weblogs will lose readers over time if its editor's focus shifts from becoming an expert to becoming a "Web personality" or if its editor becomes widely perceived as a crank.

First, Do No Harm

The reputation-building weblog is vastly more concerned with its audience than any other type. It is likely to have a less casual tone than any of the others: It is on a par with a professional meeting or even a job interview. If you are seeking to build a professional reputation, never publicly complain about your employer or your clients. In fact, I would advise you to speak only rarely—and then carefully—about your personal life, if at all. I know of one weblogger who was not hired for a job after a potential employer read earlier weblog entries complaining about a former client. Do not publish anything on a professional weblog that you would not say at a job interview.

This does not mean that you should not be yourself, just that you should consult your mental picture of your audience to determine what will and will not be appropriate. Take into consideration, for example, how your audience will react to vulgar language, or whether they will be offended by links to sites that contain off-color material. Even a weblog aimed toward model railroad enthusiasts might not link to pictures of J-Lo's latest Grammy outfit if that will create the impression that the maintainer is not serious about her rail joiners. On the other hand, if you think your fellow hobbyists don't get out much, an occasional link of this type may enhance your reputation among your constituency. When you are using your weblog to build a reputation, in all things, consult your audience's taste.

Ultimately, the purpose of your weblog is whatever you want it to be; most weblogs achieve several purposes simultaneously. The mix will depend on your circumstances and your personality. Still, it is helpful to have some idea of why keeping a weblog appeals to you. If you can't readily define your purpose, it may be helpful to take an inventory of your five favorite weblogs and ask yourself what each of them is trying to do. Or to approach it from another angle, when you imagine yourself writing your ideal weblog, what do you imagine your weblog looks like? What do you imagine your readers think about when they read your ideal weblog? Why do they come back?

Once you have an idea of your purpose, it should be easy to define your audience. If your weblog's primary mission is to fill a niche by sharing information on a defined topic, and especially if you intend to build a reputation through your work, consider whether you are writing for a professional audience or one composed of enthusiasts. Writing for a professional audience will place the greatest constraints on your subject matter, your language, and your general demeanor. Again, if your weblog is directed at a professional audience, say only what you would feel comfortable saying in any other professional situation. From now on, this website is your calling card.

Writing for friends and family will affect your writing, too. You may be reluctant to include a link to an off-color site if your grandmother reads your site regularly, and you will not want to call one of your friends a dweeb if she will be checking in later in the week.

But if your weblog is strictly personal, you have a much greater leeway in your choice of expression and subject matter. A personal weblog, even one that is ostensibly topic driven, may be forgiven for veering into exotic subject matter. If you find that your subject-specific weblog has expanded to include other topics, you might consider starting a new weblog, but unless you are determined to become known as The Expert on your topic, I would advise you simply to expand your subject matter to "whatever I'm interested in." Unless you have unlimited free time I think it would be very difficult to maintain more than one weblog (though some people do so), and in my experience one of the primary benefits of maintaining a weblog is the opportunity to discover interests you weren't fully aware of or to develop the ones you have never actively explored.

Using Your Audience

Your audience will play two roles as you create your weblog. First, keeping your audience in mind will prevent you from damaging your reputation or your relationships. Second, and even more important, awareness of your audience will force you to be better at what you do. It is your imagined audience who asks why a link is of interest or insists that you explain your point of view more fully. It is your imagined audience to whom you are describing your walk around campus ("Grandma loves birds; I'll be sure to mention that I saw a Baltimore oriole nesting in the elm tree that shades the physics lab"). Writing that you had an exceptional dinner last night won't jog even your own memory when you read the entry three months from now; but if you tell your readers that the lamb was flavored with rosemary, the potatoes whipped to silkiness, and the crème brûlée scented with rose petals, neither you nor they will wonder why you bothered to record the event.

If a friend mentions one of your entries and you find yourself telling her why you felt that link was interesting or describing the details of the incident you wrote about, you can be sure that you aren't doing your best work on your site. When you are writing, think of the questions another person would ask, or pretend you are explaining your position to someone. Imagine that you are describing the situation to a new beau, or just decide that you are writing to someone who thinks you're fascinating. Obviously, sometimes you will choose to link with only a bare description of what is on the other side. But if you do choose to comment, first take the time to understand your own point of view by using this imagined other to ask you questions about why you are linking or writing at all.

Coming Up Short

As you read and think and write daily, you will quickly find that you are smarter, more interesting, and more articulate than you ever dreamed you could be. But when you are starting out—and even when you have been doing a weblog for a while—it really can seem that everyone else is doing better work than you. It happens to me still.

When this happens, take a spin through your favorite weblogs, paying close attention to what they do and how they do it. What kinds of articles or webpages do they link? How do they structure their linktext? Do they provide extensive commentary or do they let their link choices stand on their own? Do they summarize or analyze? When they comment, are they serious, humorous, or snarky? Are they reserved about their private lives or do they speak of personal things? When they do, which details do they reveal and which do they omit? Do personal stories take place in the past or the present? Do they involve others? And the most important questions: What do you like about their weblog? What makes it fun to read? It may sound obvious, but you will become a better writer more quickly if you read and emulate the best.

Next, pick an entry that you especially enjoy and go try to do it yourself. Write some linktext or a personal entry in the voice of another weblogger, using your own material. Then try using that technique once a day for a week or two to see whether it suits you. I did this myself after reading one weblogger's complaint that others were not sufficiently summarizing their links, and his advice to use generous pull quotes. I had been more of the "clever linktext" school, and so I grumbled when I read this pronouncement, but one day I decided to try it out. For a week I constructed nearly every entry on Rebecca's Pocket by summarizing each article and following it with a pull quote. I became bored using this as a universal approach, but I learned a lot that week about when this technique worked best and how to select pull quotes for the greatest effect.

The ultimate goal of trying out and analyzing new techniques regularly is to have as many tricks in your bag as you possibly can. By trying out various techniques and even trying on other writers' voices, you will expand your own range of expression. When you experiment in this way, don't worry that you will somehow suppress your own voice. What you will learn when you write every day is this: You can't not sound like yourself. If you are taking the time to formulate your own opinions, you will not be derivative, no matter what the formal elements of the entry itself.

As you read and analyze others' work, cultivate a sense of camaraderie with the webloggers you are learning from. Do not become competitive; let others inspire you to become better than you are now. When you see an entry that is particularly well formed, spend some time deciphering what makes it work so well. When someone posts an especially obscure or intelligent link, let that inspire you to do a little old-school surfing to find one of your own. Your weblog is your playground. Keep it fun for yourself. Pretend that your audience thinks you are the most fascinating person alive, and use whatever tools you have to let them know exactly what you think about current foreign policy, your favorite brand of tofu, or your new haircut.

The Audience of One

If you allow yourself to begin posting entries based on what you think someone else wants you to write, you are missing the point of having a weblog. Even more destructive is the numbers game. It is always flattering to discover that someone else likes reading what you write, but if you begin to focus on gaining the largest audience you can, you will destroy whatever pleasure you may otherwise derive from your work. Someone will always have a larger audience than you do, and someone else will always have a larger audience than theirs. The surest way to sabotage your enjoyment of your weblog is to start caring about how many people a day look at your site. So understand that the attention you pay to your audience is not aimed at impressing them. Your only objective is to avoid sorely offending them.

This distinction is crucial. If you begin to write or link to pieces that are intended to impress your imagined audience, you will quickly become bored, and probably boring. It was once a truism that any new weblogger would, in three months' time, announce that they "needed a break" only to return a week later, proclaiming that they were no longer writing for their audience, but only for themselves. *What audience?* I would always wonder, imagining angry emails demanding "more links about dog food!" If you want to create a compelling weblog, you must write for an audience of one: yourself.

The audience of one is the single most important principle behind creating a website—or anything—that is fresh, interesting, and compelling. Consult your own taste, and then consult your audience—but only in regard to your presentation of the material. When you consider whether to add a link, first think carefully about whether it is interesting to you. If it really isn't, leave it. If it is, ask yourself why you think it is interesting or important, and then do your best to convey that in your linktext. When you sit down to update your site, write whatever is on your mind. You can edit it before you post it, or decide not to post it at all. But remember that your weblog is your play space and behave accordingly. On this page you are the king, and what is interesting to you is what is interesting to everyone. Here, your opinions are important, and everyone clamors to know what you think.

There are half a million weblogs; yours will be compelling only to the extent that it reflects your unique way of looking at the world. Your perspective is the point. It's the only reason to read a weblog at all. Do not be afraid to speak your mind. Many of us are afraid to say what we really think; but once you begin, you will find that it is refreshing and even liberating. Take advantage of the fact that you have such a space, and really take the time to say what you mean. You may want to spend some time researching your subject so that you can provide authoritative links to back up your opinion, a luxury only those with photographic memories have when debating a point in real time. Because you are writing, you have the time to get the words just right. Don't be afraid to use a thesaurus and dictionary to find the word that will most clearly express your point of view. Take your time. Think as you write, and be willing to rewrite until each sentence of each entry says exactly what you want it to.

CHALLENGE YOURSELF: Instead of linking the first account of a news story you find, take the time to search and compare several versions from different news sources, then link the one or two you think best tell the story. If you tend to read the same news sources every day, redo your news portal with some different publications on top. If you read the same blogs every day, shake it up by checking their sidebars for blogs you haven't read and add them to your rotation for a while. When you notice that another weblogger frequently finds great articles from a news source you don't usually read, consider adding it to your rotation. When a blogger posts an entry that is especially funny or moving, try building on their story by relating a similar incident from your own life.

Keep it interesting for you and your readers by making your weblog a bit of a moving target. Research a news item in more depth than usual, relate an event from your own day from the point of view of your neighbor or coworker, or spend some time searching for good links on your favorite painter or poet. If you find yourself writing a long entry, consider turning it into a full-fledged essay. Start doing what you normally do, then take it to the next level.

HAVE SOME FUN: Even if your weblog is focused on serious subjects, both you and your audience will enjoy it more if you allow yourself to play around, at least occasionally. Write an entry in haiku, open a drawer and tell a story about whatever your eye falls on, or type a stream-of-consciousness comment on a news story. If you are a programmer, add new functionality to your website; if you are a designer, redesign; if you are a writer, put up some poetry. Anything that gives you pleasure will add personality to your site, and besides, what is the point of a hobby unless it's fun?

ALLOW YOURSELF THE LUXURY OF IMPERFECTION: This is your space. In order to get good at anything, you must be willing first to do it badly. If you can't get the words quite right, put the entry up anyway. If you're not sure if anyone else will get the joke, post it immediately! (Historically, some of my funniest material is understood and appreciated only by me. And it's damn funny.) You will most enjoy writing your weblog if you approach it as your private sandbox. If, after writing and rewriting an entry, you can't quite articulate your objection to current foreign policy, post it anyway. You'll have another chance to try tomorrow or next week or next month.

Writing is often a useful way for me to get at what I'm thinking. When I write an essay I have a chance to spend time focused on a particular set of ideas, and in mulling them over I come to know more fully what I think. A weblog entry, being shorter, doesn't afford the same level of extended reflection. But over time, I may observe my thoughts beginning to take a shape. Be willing to think out loud when you are commenting on the news and on your world. You will not be perfect, ever. But by writing daily you will become a better writer and by articulating your ideas you will find out what you think.

I believe that a weblog is judged superior based on the authenticity of its voice. My prescription as outlined in this chapter is founded on three elements: challenging yourself, having fun, and most importantly, writing from the perspective that your opinion matters. The sole purpose of the weblog is to describe the world as seen through one person's eyes. That which you think is smart, interesting, idiotic, or moving is the only subject matter worthy of being placed on your site. On your weblog, your view of the world is the only one that has any bearing. I cannot say this strongly enough. Your authentic voice will come from articulating the world as you experience it, whatever that experience is. As you honestly stretch yourself to meet the world, describing it as best you can, your voice will begin to emerge. As you continue to investigate your own way of seeing things, that voice will strengthen.

This applies to collaborative and professional weblogs as much as it does to personal sites. A weblog that is maintained by a group of people will simply reflect many points of view.

On some, distinct voices will speak to the reader, one after the other; on collaborative weblogs whose members share a strong vision, individual voices will be harder to distinguish. In both cases, a new voice will emerge, that of the weblog itself, a synthesis of many viewpoints that merge to create a distinct community.

Topic-specific sites may be less personal, but they are equally subjective. Anyone can perform a daily or weekly search for news stories on a particular topic or subscribe to a headline aggregator. But it requires human judgment to sift through those results to compile a daily list of genuinely topical links. Only a knowledgeable individual will include a seemingly unrelated article because they can see the ramifications for their field, and only a well-informed person can contextualize current news with related or historical links to give their readers a fuller understanding of the significance of an event. Even the most relentlessly nonpersonal weblog has a point of view, and weblogs that provide links and no personal commentary range from the informative to the very funny. Link choice is voice, and those who say otherwise have not quite grasped the essence of hypertext.

Remember that even the strongest weblogs have days when they are rather dull, and even the most experienced webloggers become discouraged and bored with their sites. My favorite acting teacher told a story about performing brilliantly onstage one night. When a close friend came backstage after the performance she asked, "How was it?" and waited to hear the raves. Her friend said sympathetically, "It's okay, there will be other nights." Her point was that you are never the best—or even a good—judge of your own work. She taught us to focus on our task and not to waste energy worrying about the results.

Since a weblog is performed in entries instead of real time, you have the luxury of deciding when and what to post. But once it's up, don't waste any time agonizing about whether it is good enough. Put in the effort while you are creating the post, and then let it go. Insert a correction later if you make a factual error, but don't agonize about wording that doesn't completely convey your thoughts.

The distinguishing characteristic of a successful weblogger is not that she is consistently brilliant, but that she consistently updates her site, whether that be once a day or once a week. Reading a great weblog is rather like getting inside someone's brain and just poking around. The best weblogs of all types are varied, opinionated, unexpected, and incomplete.

I would encourage you to embrace all the elements at your disposal. Experiment with different forms of linktext, different lengths of entries, much commentary, no commentary. Write short. Write long. If you are so inclined, play with the design of your site. If you love to code, your site can be a project that expands as your skills grow; if you don't know anything about coding, your site may become a fantastic impetus to learn a little bit about HTML or cascading style sheets. Add photographs. Write essays. Hone your Web searching skills and publish the results. Tell stories. Be willing to experiment. Play.

The more your weblog reflects your interests and your worldview, the stronger your voice will be. Write as if your life were an exotic country, describing it as though it were unfamiliar to you. Work hard to share your unique view of the world with anyone who stumbles upon your page. Though you may think you are boring or commonplace, you are unlike anyone who has ever lived or ever will. Don't try to be different from who you are or different from anyone else; use your weblog to be more yourself every day.

Your singular way of experiencing and interpreting the world is the only thing that distinguishes you from a hundred thousand other webloggers. Use your weblog to distill your own unique way of seeing the world and to replace expected reactions with genuine response. As far as you can, remove yourself from the expectations that every life accumulates relentlessly, and instead see and think and feel with the diamond clarity that is your own. Then will your true voice sing, the voice that draws others toward you even as it teaches you who you really are.

Referenced URLs

Wood S Lot	http://www.ncf.ca/~ek867/wood_s_lot.html

Good Advice on Weblogging and Writing

Adding value to your links, Jorn Barger	http://www.robotwisdom.com/web/value.html
The Elements of Style, William Strunk, Jr.	http://www.bartleby.com/141/index.html

Voice

There are many fine writers on the Web today. This is an arbitrary and very incomplete sampling of weblogs that I think have very strong voices.

Ancient World Web	http://julen.net/ancient/breaking.html
Caught In Between	http://www.lagtime.com/cib/
Daily Brad	http://www.bradlands.com/dailybrad/index.shtml
Dollarshort	http://www.dollarshort.org/
Follow Me Here	http://gelwan.com/followme.html
Geegaw	http://www.geegaw.com/
Jish.nu	http://www.jish.nu/

Voice *(continued)*

Larkfarm	http://www.larkfarm.com/weblog.asp
Misc	http://www.miscmedia.com/
Mister Pants	http://misterpants.com/01/
rc3.org	http://www.rc3.org/
Riley Dog	http://www3.telus.net/blueplane/rileydog.html
Strange Brew	http://50cups.com/strange/index.asp
Textism	http://www.textism.com/
Waterloo Wide Web	http://www.waterlooregion.org/www/index.html
The Web Today	http://www.thewebtoday.com/
What's On It for Me?	http://www.perpetualbeta.com/weblog.html

5

Finding an Audience

Better to write for yourself and have no public than
to write for the public and have no self.

CYRIL CONNOLLY

It's natural to want an audience to read your work. You're spending one or two hours daily surfing the Web, crafting careful linktext, and deliberately expressing your thoughts and telling your stories. But there are what, half a million weblogs now? You might stand out, but how will anyone even find you? More importantly, how will the right people find your new weblog? You can take a number of simple steps to help them out. Let's start with the obvious ones first.

Obvious Strategies

REGISTERING YOUR WEBSITE: When seeking to publicize their site, the first thing most people think of is registering their website with the most popular Web directories and search engines.

A Web portal or directory is a listing of websites, usually organized into categories. Yahoo! is probably the best-known example. Additionally, these directories often allow you to "search the Web." Interestingly, the results you get from searching one of these sites are usually different from the ones you would get from following links from their top pages deep into their various categories. In other words, searching for "weblog" on Yahoo! will bring you a different set of links than you will find by drilling down from their homepage to the "weblogs" category: "Home – Social Science – Communications – Writing – Journals and Diaries – Online Journals and Diaries – Web Logs." Generally, Web directories allow website owners to submit sites to be considered for inclusion.

There are websites devoted to explaining how to submit and optimize your site for these services (check the end of this chapter), and they can explain the ins and outs more thoroughly than I can here.

If you're interested, it's worth spending a Saturday afternoon on this, but I doubt you'll get much traffic from these portals. There was a time when Web portals were happy to add more sites to their directories, but I don't think anyone anticipated the growth of the Web or the number of websites that eventually would be submitted daily. To my knowledge, no one has yet figured out how to make much money with a Web portal. These sites are faced with more submissions than they can handle, a small staff to sort through them, and the prospect of losing money from the venture. This means several things to you.

1. After you submit your URL, it will take days, weeks, or even months before your site shows up in the directory (although you may show up through a search before then). Without spending some money, there is nothing you can do to speed this up. Just be patient.

2. When submitting your site, you will be pointed first to paid placement; these portal businesses are desperate to make money through any means possible. In some cases you are paying for placement, and in others you are paying for "expedited consideration"—meaning that you may only have paid to be rejected sooner! Don't ever pay to have your website listed in a Web directory. It will never, ever be worth it. I think I've received fewer than a dozen hits from

any portal since I began Rebecca's Pocket three and a half years ago. Submit your site to Web directories, but only to those that allow you to do so for free.

3. Understand that you may *never* be listed on a given Web portal, and there's nothing you can do about it. Don't let it bother you. I've submitted Rebecca's Pocket at least three times to Yahoo! and they have yet to include me. Though I followed their directions carefully, and they list many weblogs that are much younger than mine, Yahoo! just won't add me to their list. Why? Who knows? I guess they don't like the cut of my jib. It really doesn't matter. My traffic continues to grow steadily without them and so will yours.[1]

4. In Web articles about optimizing your website for search engines, you will read about the importance of metatags. Spend as much or as little time on them as you desire. Many weblogs, especially those maintained by Web professionals, include metatags, and, indeed, their creators would not dream of creating a website without them. Conversely, though I keep meaning to do it, I've never gotten around to adding metatags to Rebecca's Pocket, and my site is crawled by all of the major search engines. At the time of this writing, a search for "rebecca" using AltaVista (which, according to Search Engine Watch, uses metatags in compiling their listings) returns Rebecca's Pocket as both of the top two results. My understanding is this: Metatags *might* improve your listing with some search engines, and they definitely *will not* with others. If you are using your weblog as a means to learn more about HTML and Web design, by all means spend the time to learn how to create metatags so that you can easily add them to the sites you make professionally.

---

[1] In a senseless twist of fate, Rebecca's Pocket was finally added to the Yahoo! directory three days after I wrote this chapter. I may never forgive them. Meanwhile, I can report to you that my weblog has received approximately three hits a month from their directory (I am, after all, an "R"). Not worth losing sleep over.

Otherwise, the time you spend should be directly related to the amount of satisfaction you get from doing so.

Here's what you need to know: Search engine results can be a great source of hits, but they do not necessarily build your audience. More than one person has found my site while searching for "Laura Bush Naked" (it's a wicked, wicked world). When they don't find naked pictures of anyone, I don't imagine that they stick around for long or ever come back. The same goes for Web directories. It's nice to see your site listed, but very few people go first to a Web directory to try to find a weblog to read. Submit your site if you feel like it, then forget about it.

WEBRINGS: Webrings are designed to make it easy to surf a number of related sites, and they are one way of aligning yourself with others in your community. I've never been part of one, and I rarely use them, but webrings exist throughout the Web, so they must be popular. A member site will have a set of links that look something like this: << clevername webring >>. "Clevername" will, surprisingly, be a clever name that gives you some indication as to what all of the sites have in common: webloggers or GLBT webloggers or Aussie webloggers or webloggers with a limp; something that binds them together, and that presumably may be interesting to you. Clicking on the arrows to the right and left of the name will take you forward and backward through the list, providing you with an easy surf through a circle of related sites. If one of the sites you love is a member of a webring, take a look at the other members. If you feel a kinship with them, by all means join! A webring may or may not add to your traffic, but it is a good way of aligning yourself with a cluster of related sites.

WEBLOG MAILING LISTS AND DISCUSSION GROUPS: These spring up from time to time, then seem to die. Check to see which lists are still active and if they are discussing anything that interests you. If a list is active and interesting, take some time to read past postings. This will introduce you to the scope of topics, prevent you from introducing a previously talked-to-death subject, and give you a sense of list etiquette. It's unlikely that any list will consider a message containing only your URL and an invitation to visit your site a real contribution to the conversation, but you can raise awareness of your presence in the Web community with a friendly letter of introduction and your intelligent participation in ongoing discussions. Search community group sites like Yahoo! Groups to see if there are groups devoted to weblogs.

UPDATE TRACKERS: Several services are available that provide a listing of recently updated weblogs. Some generate these directories by checking their list of weblogs at intervals, and others require that the weblog maintainer notify the service. Some of the newer weblog management tools can be set to automatically notify these services whenever you update your weblog; if you use one of them, you need do nothing else. If you maintain your site by hand or use a tool that does not include such a feature, you may still be able to notify these sites manually. Check the site to see how the listings are created.

Trackers are a popular way to surf weblogs, and many webloggers find themselves using them more frequently than they do their own portals. These sites generate the most click-throughs for weblogs that already have name recognition. If you want more traffic to your site, by all means participate, but don't rely on these services alone to generate interest in your site. The audience that comes to your site through these services will likely have already read your site or heard your name elsewhere.

Building Your Online Presence

SIGFILES: Once you've made your weblog public, you should immediately add your URL to your sigfile. You've seen sigfiles: the chunk of information at the end of an email. Professionals often include their name, title, and contact information in their sigfile, attached automatically by their email program whenever they send a message. Add the URL of your weblog to your personal email account to remind your correspondents that you are now keeping a weblog. (If you don't know how to do this, open your email program and search the help files for "signature" or "signatures" and then follow the directions.)

Some people set their sigfile to automatically include their usual closing, some add quotations, and others just add their URL. Your sigfile may look something like this:

----

http://www.rebeccablood.net/

In a situation where there is no righteous person,
try to be a righteous person.   - Hillel

What matters is that your URL be included beneath your signature on every email you send out. Whether or not you notified your friends when you started your weblog, from now on, every email you send will be an advertisement for your website. Be sure to begin your URL with **http://** ; if you don't, some email programs won't recognize it as a link.

LISTSERVS: The Internet is full of listservs (electronic mailing lists) on almost any topic you can think of. You may belong to a few already. Participating on a listserv is another avenue for building your online reputation, in this case with your intelligent and considerate contributions to the list.

If you already belong to a mailing list, you will want to continue participating as you have been, with the all-important addition of your sigfile to the messages you contribute. Do not announce your weblog to the list, unless you are maintaining a subject-specific weblog pertinent to the list topic. Using a topic-centered discussion group or listserv to promote your business or personal webpage is an abuse of the system. It will irritate other members, and may even result in your removal from the list.

If you do not belong to any mailing lists but you would like to try one out, find one that genuinely interests you. There is no point in cluttering up your mailbox with messages on an uninteresting topic. After subscribing to any listserv, you will receive a note explaining how to unsubscribe and set your preferences for the list. Save it! You will need it if (when) you decide to leave. I filter all of my listserv mail into separate folders, and I save that first message into the folder with the rest of the mail from the list. If you tend to purge old email frequently, save that initial email in a folder called "save" or "listservs." You will need it again.

Read the list for a week (or several) before you begin posting. Your purpose is to begin building name recognition so that people will be more inclined to read your weblog. That means that you are here to make a good impression, so you will want to understand community standards before you jump in. On any listserv, it is polite to send messages only in plain text (as opposed to HTML) and to use a sigfile that is no more than four lines long. Remember that upper case means that YOU ARE YELLING AT EVERYONE, and to use smileys when you mean to be funny. :) If you initiate a conversation, choose a subject line that is short but descriptive so that other list members can see at a glance whether or not they want to read the messages on that topic.

If the mailing list has guidelines or a frequently asked questions list (FAQ), read it! This will save you the embarrassment of having another member point you to them in response to one of your first queries to the list.

If you will be away from your computer for a week or more, consider unsubscribing from the list so that you do not have to wade through (or more likely, delete) every message that comes through while you are away. If you use an auto responder to automatically reply to messages while you are away, you *must* unsubscribe from all of your mailing lists; otherwise your auto-respond message will go out to the list, come into your mailbox, back out to the list, back into your mailbox, literally ad infinitum. People *will* remember your name if this happens, but not in a good way. If you haven't been unsubscribed by the list administrator while you were gone, you will surely be so embarrassed that you will do so yourself when you get home.

Keep in mind that any listserv that archives its messages on the Web is recording your words for all posterity . . . and the post you make today will appear tomorrow when someone does a search for your name. You are creating an online reputation, and thoughtless words may come back to haunt you.

Do not feel that you must post a message daily or even weekly. It is better to send an intelligent, thoughtful note once a month than to send drivel to the list every day. Unless you are providing quick, specific answers on a list that is focused on information sharing, do not send more than one or two notes a day. Remember, too, that even if you rarely respond publicly, these forums can be excellent sources for interesting links and inside information. Exceptional links often move through my listservs straight onto my weblog. If I wouldn't have seen the article without the listserv, I can reasonably assume that most of my readers have not seen it either.

In general, behave as you would at any social gathering: Take the time to gauge the mood and manners of the group, do not hog the conversation, listen and respond respectfully to differing points of view, and share information generously.

Joining Community Sites: These range from community websites like Plastic and MetaFilter to personal websites with discussion areas. The rules you will follow on these sites are similar to the mailing list etiquette discussed above. Read the site for a week or two to get a sense of the site. Every community has its own rules and standards. What is de rigueur at Mardi Gras may not be acceptable at a Quaker meeting, so pay attention to where the lines are drawn. As with mailing lists, your goal is to find a site filled with like-minded people, and then to fit into the community. Trying to remake any community in your own image will only alienate current members, and possibly get you kicked out altogether.

You may choose to follow and participate in only one or two threads a day or week; you may find that you gain more from the community by lurking than by actively posting; and you must always remember that your words are the only measure other members have of you. Readers will form their entire impression of you based on the things you contribute, and those contributions, forever preserved in the site archives, will continue to be the sole means by which others come to know you, possibly long after your interest in a particular community has waned. If you hope to excite interest in your weblog, you will have to interact with others in an interesting and friendly way. Listen respectfully, have fun, and be yourself.

Online Rules of the Road

Remember, everything you say online is creating a persona, and every persona carries with it a reputation. Take care to create an impression that you can be proud of. If you want to create an active presence in an online forum, community site, or listserv—and especially if you want to debate a highly charged topic—here are a few steps you can take to make sure that doing so enhances your reputation rather than damaging it.

1. Do not post when you are angry. Period.
2. Always argue the facts, never the personalities. There is a big difference between "The facts don't support that interpretation of this event" and "That's a stupid thing to say"—

or worse, "I can't believe how stupid you are." If you want to argue a point, be willing to back it up with facts, ideally with links to online sources.

3. Once you have stated your arguments as clearly and cogently as you can, sit back and read what others have to say—you may learn something. There is nothing wrong with posting several notes in defense of your opinion, but after three or four notes, it's probably best to pass the talking stick to someone else. Don't be afraid to ask questions if you are unclear about something. In fact, this can be an effective way to engage an individual with a different view, as it indicates your willingness to learn more about the topic and to hear them out.

4. Respond to personal attacks by ignoring them. Bring the conversation back to the issue at hand and argue the facts. If someone steps far over the line, you may neutrally point out that the offending remarks are of a personal nature, but don't respond in kind. Don't allow anyone to draw you into a flamewar; doing so risks your credibility, raises your blood pressure, and wastes your time.

5. Do not hijack conversations. If you find a second conversation developing within another, create a new subject heading to reflect the new topic so that community members may choose which thread to follow. If you are posting to a community site on which you cannot change the topic, start a new thread. Above all, if things begin to get silly, but others continue diligently to pursue the original topic of conversation, don't clutter up a thread with nonsense: You will be seen as part of the problem.

6. Do not misrepresent other people's positions. Always do your best to understand other members' points of view and respond to them respectfully and accurately. Astute readers will see you as belligerent or stupid if you consistently argue against positions that your opponents do not hold.

It is acceptable in most communities to disagree with other members but only if your disagreement is courteous, well-supported, and never veers into personal attacks. If you are rude you will not be well regarded, and your credibility in general will suffer.

Building Your Community Presence

PROVIDING A SERVICE: What do you have to share with the online community? Some webloggers regularly provide coding tips, free postcards, or desktop wallpaper. If you feel that you are an expert user of a particular weblog tool or other commonly used software, consider offering tutorials on your site or providing advice in user forums. Individuals all over the Web have built their reputations by generously sharing their expertise with the community at large. These people are not concerned about making money with their websites; they are dedicated to helping others gain expertise and to making the Web better for everyone. The Web is a genuine gift economy, and you will gain personal currency the more you give away.

JOINING COMMUNITY EVENTS: Webloggers often organize community-wide events. Probably the most successful of these to date has been "Link and Think," an annual observation by webloggers and journalers of World AIDS Day, December 1, organized by Brad L. Graham of The BradLands. The event has grown from a few hundred participants to a few thousand in just three years. Other events are on a smaller scale: In September 2000, Garret Vreeland organized "Behind the Curtain," which invited webloggers to photographically document a typical day in their lives in order to give their audiences (and each other) a glimpse of the individuals behind the sites. And each Friday many webloggers answer the "Friday Five."

Participating in events like these will bring you at least a little traffic immediately following the event. If it does nothing else, it will bring you to the attention of the other participants. If an event moves you or looks interesting, join in; if it leaves you cold, don't. Joining a larger event can give you a nice sense of belonging to a larger group, but will not necessarily bring you many visitors, since the list of participants will be long; by participating in smaller events your name will be more prominent, but the event itself may not have widespread recognition.

Occasionally, someone will organize a regional meeting of webloggers, or a traveling weblogger may announce that he will be in town and is looking for dinner partners or seeking to organize a larger gathering. By all means, attend! This is a fantastic way to put faces to weblogs, and these gatherings are always fun. Even if you are uncomfortable meeting new people (as I usually am), make yourself go; bring a friend (even a non-weblogger) if you have to. The people who attend these events are, in my experience, uniformly nice, and the fact that all of you read and write weblogs gives you something in common.

If you have time to make business cards for your site before you attend, do it. They can be simple, with just your weblog name, email address, and URL. Business cards are inexpensive, will remind attendees of your URL when they get home, and they give you something to do immediately upon meeting everyone. If you can, read the weblogs of those people you know will be attending, since this will give you some ready topics of conversation. Most people will be flattered if you offer a comment on something they linked, and you will have some idea of the range of interests of the people you are going to meet. Don't be embarrassed if your weblog isn't well-known; everyone started with an unknown site.

If you are usually uncomfortable in social situations, list a few questions in your head beforehand. Fellow attendees' weblogs will offer you clues to their interests and circumstances: Have you just read an article on their favorite topic? How is their car running? If you are meeting an out-of-towner, how was their trip? What are they in town for? If they are local, how long have they lived here? When and why did they move here?

Remember that people love to talk about their interests and themselves. If anyone seems reluctant to give personal details, ask them questions about their interests or their weblog. If you are surrounded by a group of avid conversationalists, you can just enjoy listening to them carry on. But I encourage you to take advantage of any opportunity to meet your weblogging colleagues. When you get home, send a short email to whoever you liked talking with, telling them how much you enjoyed meeting them. It really can be no more than that, and people will remember your good manners.

Making Connections

THE GENUINE FAN EMAIL: The keys here are "genuine" and "fan." Sending a note to a popular weblogger whose site you don't usually read will rarely inspire their interest. Few things are less compelling than a note that says "Check out my site!" Even worse is the note that goes on for three paragraphs about the author's credentials and intelligence, and then invites you to come bask in the glow of his new weblog.

But there are two types of notes that may help bring you to the attention of a weblogger you admire. The first is a specific response to something he has posted on his site. Even if he isn't actively soliciting feedback, a note providing an additional piece of information or your comment on a particular entry will let him know that his work has inspired a thoughtful response. The other is a general note of appreciation, a note saying that you admire his weblog. It can be a few lines or a few paragraphs, but everyone enjoys hearing that their hard work is appreciated.

If you do choose to send another weblogger a note, don't be disappointed if you don't receive a reply. Everyone you email is maintaining their weblog in their spare time. While some webloggers are scrupulous about answering all their email, some simply don't have time to do so. If it is a choice between updating their weblog, answering your note, or maintaining their marriage (or even going to get a beer with some friends), most people are going to put your note last on the list. This doesn't mean that they didn't read and appreciate your note. Likely they clicked through the URL in your sigfile to see what your weblog was about, even if they didn't have time to answer you.

LINKING TO OTHERS: Many beginning webloggers don't realize it, but any website can monitor its traffic to tell which sites its visitors came from. When you link to another site, each time a person clicks that link, the maintainer of the other site will find your URL (the referrer) in their daily server logs. Most webloggers check their referrer logs frequently, and human nature almost guarantees that they will check out a new site that has linked to them. This is probably the single most effective strategy for politely announcing your presence as a new member of the community.

You may already include the traditional sidebar of other weblogs on your site, or you may have created a portal page. Reading over any weblogger's sidebar is like perusing their bookshelves; it tells you what they're interested in and whom they admire. Since you are writing and linking about what interests you, there is a good chance that the kinds of things you write about will be interesting to the weblog editors you admire. Even if another weblog does not find your site compelling, they will think well of your good taste.

Scrupulously crediting other weblogs for the links you find on theirs serves a similar purpose. When this happens, you have an opportunity to comment on a story or article they have already deemed interesting enough to offer to their readers, and they may find your commentary to be equally interesting. Most of the time you will want only to link the article, write your linktext, and at the end of the entry note: (found via example.com). When a weblogger finds your site in his referrers, he may click through to see why you linked to his site. When he sees the "via" link, he will think you are polite and interested in interesting things, and he will enjoy seeing his site linked on your page.

There are two reasons to link to other weblogs. The first is to create awareness of your weblog within the community. Just getting your name out there is a first step to being remembered. The second is the hope that eventually the weblogs you link to will link back. They may find an article through your weblog and credit you with a "via" link. They may find so many interesting articles or like your writing so well that they add you to their portal. Even when a weblogger does not link you, he may click through when your weblog is listed on an update tracker or linked on another site.

However, when you link to any other weblog, do not waste your energy being offended if they do not link back. Some of the weblogs I most admire have never linked to me, and probably never will. Others with which I see very little commonality, do. Sometimes a weblogger no longer uses his own portal to surf weblogs or does not have time to update his links; sometimes he has only limited time for surfing, and adding another site to his list is impractical. Sometimes he simply is not very interested in what you have to say. His reasons may have everything to do with you, or they may have nothing to do with you. Accept it and move on.

A final word on this strategy: When you link to another weblog, always click the link! You cannot rely on your readers to click through the links on your sidebar (which is there, after all, primarily for your convenience) and relatively few people click "via" links. Even in cases where a link is the featured point of an entry, in my experience only about one out of every ten visitors will click through. Don't be a voice crying in the wilderness. Put your daily entries onto the Web, and then click through to every other weblog you cite.

CROSS-BLOG TALK: A variation on the "via" link is the cross-blog entry, in which you link to another weblogger's comment in order to build on what he has said or offer a different view. In either case, your reaction will be to the weblogger's commentary, not to an outside source. Some people find these entries hopelessly recursive, but for others this "cross-blog talk" is of the highest value.

Naturally, you should have something interesting to say, additional facts to offer, or another perspective. No one will find such an entry worthwhile if all you do is to link to another weblog entry with the words "Right on, Nicholas!" Keep in mind that Nicholas may not choose to link to your comments or to carry the thought further in public—he may have nothing to add—but if he finds your comments interesting he may visit your site in the future.

If Nicholas's weblog allows reader comments, consider making your comment there. If your comments are interesting and on-topic, readers will be interested in learning more about the person who made them and may click through to your site.

Some readers dislike cross-blog talk, but as long as you have something thoughtful to say about another weblogger's commentary, most of them will tolerate it. Don't expect a weblogger who doesn't regularly engage in this type of exchange to respond publicly to your comments.

Strategies That May Backfire

CROSS-BLOG SOCIALIZING: There is another form of cross-blog talk that I should mention here—discussion between weblogs that is not focused on an exchange of ideas but is instead a form of small talk. I call this cross-blog socializing, and it is irresistible to many new webloggers, who are fascinated and delighted with the community they have joined. Mentioning other webloggers merely to mention them, or in the hope that they will in turn link to you, is fine, but be aware that if your weblog largely consists of comments to other webloggers—even two or three a day—you will severely limit your potential audience.

If you love your new community and find an engaging group of people who love to socialize virtually, that's exactly what you should do. But your audience is likely to consist primarily of these other webloggers, who are, naturally, the most interested in this talk. Even readers who find cross-blog talk about ideas to be of high value tend to be uninterested in these public social interactions.

TALKING ABOUT A REVOLUTION: Similarly, constant talk about weblogs and weblogging is tedious for almost everyone else. Every medium loves to reflect upon itself, and weblogs are no exception. But what seems like a fascinating subject to practitioners can be deadly boring to others. If you are fascinated with weblogs but don't want to limit your readership to a small subset of other equally fascinated webloggers, research and think about the subject, then put it together in occasional longer pieces. Interested readers will click through to read the essay; importantly, because your weblog has been focused on other subjects, you will *have* readers who don't keep their own weblogs. Again, a weblog about weblogging is fine if that's your passion, but know that your audience will be limited.

BECOMING NOTORIOUS: Back in the day, when the weblog community consisted of fewer than a hundred people, a few people gained everyone's full attention with practical jokes and weblog entries that were designed to get a rise from other members of the community. Everyone else watched to see whether those who had been publicly tweaked would publicly squeak or simply ignore the whole affair. The reactions were generally predictable: The blowhards blew, the good-humored chuckled, and the dignified ignored it all.

It can't be done today. There are simply too many weblogs, and there is no one weblog that is known by all of them. There are certainly weblog clusters—amorphous, undefined groups of weblogs that tend to link to one another and share a general set of interests and worldview. But these tend to be groups of twenty or thirty, and they have chosen their alignment with one another. Such a stunt would only alienate the very people whose attention you wished to attract. Becoming notorious worked for two or three people in 1999 because the community had enlarged to the point that it was somewhat impersonal, but it was still small enough that everyone knew everyone else's personality. It will never work that way again.

Most of those notorious weblogs have faded from view. Being mean isn't that fun after a while, and how many ways can you poke fun at the same few people? Being mean gets boring for your audience, too, and thinking up new ways to tweak people must become tiresome. And I suspect it's counter to the reasons you began weblogging in the first place.

I began because I fell in love with the weblog, and I thought I had something to say. I admired the people whose sites I read and I wanted to be respected by them in return. I still feel that way. What you publish will follow you, and alienating others is a poor strategy for gaining the continued attention and eventual regard of the people whose sites you eagerly read every day. You will gain status by speaking truthfully on your weblog, contributing positively to the larger online community, and strengthening the weblog community in any way you can.

The strategies I've outlined fall roughly into two categories: gaining the attention of other webloggers and building your online reputation in general. If you have interesting things to say, direct exposure to the online community through participation in public forums will provide you with a small, steady source of traffic. When you participate in these forums, always think of the kind of person whose respect you want to earn, and speak to them. Posting provocatively may induce people to click through to your website, but perhaps not people of like mind. Go too far over the line, and those people who likely would enjoy the things you have to say will avoid your site altogether, having already formed a negative opinion of your personality.

Gaining the attention of other webloggers is more than an attempt to siphon their audience to your site. The inclusion of your weblog on another weblogger's sidebar or in a "via" link will probably bring you only one to five hits a day, rarely more. What matters is getting your name in front of another community of readers, whether or not they choose to explore your site. More importantly, that link lets them know that a weblogger they trust has looked at your site; since he is building his reputation on the quality of his ideas and links, that link has his tacit approval. Every experienced weblog reader knows that the best way to find good weblogs is to follow the links from the sidebar of their favorites. Even a reader who is disinclined to click through "via" links may do so if he finds your weblog referenced more than once on the weblogs he likes best.

Of course, the most personal reason for seeking the attention of the weblog community is simple: peer recognition. Being linked by one of your favorite weblogs is a lot like having an author you admire walk up at a party and say, "Hey, I really liked your last short story." It just feels great. The first time you see your weblog unexpectedly linked on another site you will blink, read the link over again to make sure you're seeing it right, and then—I guarantee it—click the link to see where it goes!

Building Your Audience

I have spent a lot of time on this subject because I feel it is natural for any writer to want readers. None of us would put it on the Web if all we wanted to do was to write. Unless your site is password protected, once you link to another site, your weblog is public. I have outlined here a number of effective strategies that might otherwise be overlooked by the novice weblogger. But I have left the three most important points for the end.

The first point is the most important: It is better to have the right audience than a large audience. Would you rather have a thousand readers a day, all of whom came once and never returned, or twenty readers who look forward every day to your weblog? Gaining an audience for your weblog is a lot like dating. You need to get your site in front of a lot of people in order to find the few who will appreciate your work. I would not trade my readers for any in the world. The notes I receive tell me that they are thoughtful, intelligent, and open-minded—just the kind of people I enjoy spending time with. Your goal is to attract a core audience of readers in tune with your way of seeing the world. Their number is irrelevant.

Second, your weblog will ultimately be judged on its merits alone, and the savviest publicity seeking cannot change that. It will do no good to concentrate your efforts on the strategies listed above if you are not giving your best effort daily on your weblog. Some days will be better than others, sure. But the weblogs that appear again and again on the sidebars of other weblogs are there because their editors put their hearts onto the page day after day, not because they worked the system better than everyone else. There is no cabal, but there are good writers, individuals with unique and thoughtful perspectives, and collectors who consistently dig up the best links.

You may feel that a few universally lauded weblogs seem quite lackluster in comparison to many others, while many, many excellent weblogs seem to have acquired only modest audiences. But ultimately you cannot choose your audience; your audience chooses you. All you can do is show up every day, writing and linking the things that entertain and move you. Trying to be like the "popular kids," you risk being derivative. Writing what you believe others want to read, you guarantee your unoriginality. Those who gain large audiences are those who return again and again to their own sense of what is interesting. Those who relentlessly challenge themselves (and thus their audiences) will find that the readers who return to their sites really want to know what they think. Those willing to be themselves cannot help surprising and delighting the rest of us with their observations and revelations.

Finally, the truth is that building an audience takes time, and it's a slow, sometimes discouraging process. When you begin, you will have an audience of one: yourself. Even your friends may not be as enthusiastic about your new venture as you think they should be. When I began my weblog, I imagined that my friends would be relieved to be free of the endless stream of email containing links I thought were interesting. "Now you can come look at my weblog whenever you want to," I told them, "and see it all at your convenience!" It took me less than a week to realize that they weren't reading my weblog at all. When I wanted to be sure that my friends saw an item, I was reduced to emailing them the link with a pathetic little reminder that it had been "linked on my weblog today." After a while, they began checking my site a few times a week (or so they tell me), but it was months before it became part of their routine.

My audience has grown steadily, but slowly. When I began tracking my traffic I was receiving a few hundred visitors a day. Then I got a big break. In July 2000 I was a featured guest on a National Public Radio show about weblogging. I think I drew a thousand unique visitors that day, and close to that number the next. I was just thrilled and dreamed that I had hit the weblog big time, that as those people told their friends my numbers would grow and grow until I was a personal publishing phenomenon with the influence of a nationally syndicated columnist. As the week passed, each day's numbers dwindled and a month later I had realized a net gain of about seventy-five regular readers, which I welcomed—but it wasn't the increase I had anticipated.

What happened was simple. Many of the people who listened to the show were intrigued enough to look at my site, but most of them did not find anything interesting enough ever to visit again. And so it has gone. A mention in a newspaper article generates fewer than ten click-throughs. A link on a popular site will bring a brief jump in traffic, most of which never returns. It is not a reflection on you. It is some combination of the exposure your site has received, your subject matter, and the amount of time the average reader has available for another piece of media. Again and again, I decide that my audience has hit some sort of natural limit, and in a few months it increases a little more.

The most reliable way to gain traffic is through a link on another weblog. People who click through to your site from another weblog are already weblog readers. They may not mind adding another to their daily rotation. A link from another weblogger serves as a kind of recommendation to their audience.

If your objective in keeping a weblog is to gain a wide audience, I advise you to quit today. Webloggers who care about the size of their audience are always unhappy. They never have the audience they think they deserve, and they always imagine that someone else does. I can't say it strongly enough: If you let yourself really care about the size of your audience, you will always be unhappy. Remember, the most popular weblogger's readership does not approach that of a student columnist at a medium-sized university newspaper. No weblog has a built-in audience base, and if your aim is to reach as many people as possible, investigate writing for your community or college newspaper, either of which will put you in front of a guaranteed number of readers every day or week.

If you are going to keep a weblog, it must be for the joy of writing alone. You will never have enough readers, and if that matters, you will always be disappointed. Weblog audiences grow very slowly, but the readers you attract come deliberately. Do what you can to deserve their attention, and accept that your audience may always be very small. Through your efforts you can hope to gain a few readers and the respect of your peers. Do your best because you love it, appreciate the readers who visit, and don't allow your statistics to ruin your fun.

Referenced URLs

Yahoo!	http://www.yahoo.com/
Search Engine Watch	http://searchenginewatch.com/
AltaVista	http://www.altavista.com/
Yahoo! Groups	http://groups.yahoo.com/
Plastic	http://www.plastic.com/
Link and Think	http://www.linkandthink.org/
The BradLands	http://www.bradlands.com/weblog/index.shtml
Behind the Curtain	http://web.archive.org/web/20011204191200/http://www.zopesite.com/behindthecurtain/
Friday Five	http://www.fridayfive.org/

6

Weblog Community and Etiquette

Live never to be ashamed if anything you do or say is published around the world—even if what is published is not true.

RICHARD BACH

The weblog community, when it began, was a cohesive unit. I think most webloggers felt a strong identification with every other weblogger, even when their interests and tastes differed in every way. The very earliest webloggers had maintained their sites for months if not years before they were named "weblogs." But with that naming, a community was created. Everyone made note when a new weblog was uncovered or created. For these writers, discovering a new weblog must have been like finding a long lost brother in the wilderness; for the readers, it was just fun.

When I started Rebecca's Pocket, there were between fifty and one hundred weblogs in all—too many for anyone to follow closely, but few enough that everyone noticed when a new name was added to the list. At the time I felt vaguely ashamed for jumping in so late in the game. But then the first weblog management tools appeared, and in just a few months I was considered one of the old-timers. The number of weblogs exploded. Suddenly no one had any idea how many weblogs were in existence or could hope to have seen even half of them. Weblog clusters emerged as webloggers converted their sidebars from more general lists of "other weblogs" to "other weblogs like mine."

Since then these clusters have enlarged and divided, then divided again. Some are very specific. If you have a weblog on any aspect of Web design, you can use your sidebar to align yourself with half a dozen different specialties within the profession. Other clusters join weblogs with similar political views or a common design aesthetic. When any group of weblogs includes the same few sites in their sidebar, you can be sure you're looking at a weblog cluster.

When I look at my portal page, I feel like I'm looking at "the weblog community" or a fair representation thereof. In fact, that assumption is entirely untrue. I'm looking at a fair representation of a specific cluster, in my case a group of sites that share my political and cultural interests, and some of the webloggers I know personally. When I take an evening to explore a random selection of unfamiliar weblogs, I am always startled to learn of large, well-developed clusters whose sidebars contain not one weblog I know.

If we are going to speak of the weblog community, it's important to realize that there is a whole weblog universe that you likely have not explored. Your cluster represents your neighborhood, the people most likely to see your work. Take a look at almost anyone's list of weblogs and you'll see that most of them are related to one another by some combination of geography, the software they use to maintain their site, and a few core weblogs in their sidebars.

Though the weblog community is widely dispersed, conventions have evolved that are shared by almost all of its members. In general, etiquette in the weblog world is based on the same principles as it is in the physical world: Common sense and courtesy rule the day.

Things to Avoid

Let's start with the things you should not do. Naturally, it's your site, and you can publish whatever you like, but if you want to gain the respect of the people you respect, you will at least want to avoid offending them, just as you would in real life. Most of these rules seem like common sense, but I have seen them broken often enough that I think they are worth mentioning.

ATTACKING OTHERS: One way to get another weblogger's attention (and possibly the attention of others) is to attack her. I don't mean a respectful disagreement with her opinion on U.S. foreign policy; I'm talking about outright attacks that seem grounded in a personal dislike for the victim. Even if your victim is known as a bully within the weblog community, this is unconscionable behavior and will make you few friends. Oh, your victim and others may link to your site and you will potentially draw quite an audience for a few days—many people can't resist watching a train wreck. But in the end the gapers will go their own way and you will be left with a reputation as being irrational or a bully; readers from outside the weblog community will find your behavior incomprehensible and will move to sites that focus on subjects they find interesting.

This is an extreme case. But even relatively mild criticism of another weblogger or her site design will reflect very unfavorably on you. Linking to another site simply to make a negative comment is analogous to walking into a party and announcing within earshot that another guest's dress is hideous or joining a conversation to advise one of the participants that he is a dimwit for complaining when his MG breaks down. Making the remark without linking the other weblog compounds rudeness with cowardice. Even if your remarks don't get back to the victim (and they probably will), thinking readers will see you as a bully and a boor.

Again, I'm not counseling against thoughtful criticism of another weblogger's political opinions or her editorial stance on the proliferation of trees with fuzzy pink flowers in her part of town. A public site invites scrutiny. Most people who offer opinions about current events are interested in, or at least not offended by, a respectful dissenting view. But unsolicited personal attacks are poor form and will win you few fans.

The rules are a little different for blog-style weblogs, though respect is still the operating principle. Blogs link to one another quite frequently, but by and large their purpose in linking is to reference the individual or to comment on or compliment a clever entry or well-written piece; but it would be uncouth to publicly offer criticism about a particularly heartfelt or personal entry.

Perhaps that seems a bit inconsistent, but again it is analogous to real life. You might announce to your workmates that the receptionist told you a hilarious story or eloquently articulated her concerns about the use of animals in medical research. But if she shared something very emotional or very personal with you—the breakup of her seven-year relationship or the account of a pet's death, and her tearful admission of regret for not spending enough time petting the fine old fellow—it would be uncouth to shout across the room to some coworkers, "Hey guys, come on over! You have to hear this story!"

In the world of weblogs similar rules apply. A respectful pointer to a heartfelt story or a link that says, "Antoinette is having a hard time" is just fine; so is a personal email expressing your support. But a link to such an entry accompanied by a callous post that says, "Antoinette finally broke up with that loser she was dating. I could never figure out how such a smart girl ended up as such a doormat" is unnecessary and rude.

Occasionally you will witness the situation I'm describing: One weblogger will make a questionable remark about another. Sometimes it begins very innocently with an off-hand remark that probably was not intended to be insulting in any way. The object of this (only marginally insulting) remark will take offense, point to the entry, and become outraged and indignant. Others jump to the allegedly attacked weblogger's defense and mount retaliatory assaults of their own. The original poster, discovering she is the cause of all this fuss, is first surprised and then offended at the slings being hurled her way and mounts a counterattack. Her friends pile on and the madness spreads, finally dissipating when everyone tires of the whole affair.

These incidents are like brushfires, spreading rapidly and dying down as quickly as they flame up. I don't know that they've become more rare, but I can say that, thankfully, I have witnessed fewer of them in the past year than I did in each of the two years before; I suspect that the community has become so widespread that when these incidents occur they are more likely to be outside the range of my sensors. My policy on dealing with weblog flamewars is simple: Ignore them. First of all, if you have any readers from outside the weblog community, they really don't want to witness the infighting. Second, in very few cases is there even a point to weighing in on the furor: None of the participants are going to change their minds. Furthermore, by taking sides you risk making an enemy over a situation that defines the phrase "tempest in a teapot."

When I feel most strongly that someone has behaved badly, I have an even more compelling reason for ignoring such behavior: I don't want to reward it. Why should I send traffic to someone who is displaying antisocial behavior? In the world of weblogs, click-throughs are currency, and I choose to vote with my links. Just as I would not patronize a grocer who spends his days calling out racial epithets to passersby, I decline to drive traffic to anyone I perceive to be insulting to others in the community.

Does this all sound incredibly petty? It is. These are high school politics played over middle school issues. Don't bother becoming involved. It's not worth the energy, you may gain the ill-will of a portion of the community, and you have absolutely nothing to gain.

This is not to imply that the weblog community is largely composed of socially impaired individuals. I don't think that's the case. But, as in any small community, whether it be a school, a club, or an office, it's easy to sometimes lose perspective. Most everyone is doing their weblog in their spare time, and those who keep at it do so because they love it. Most of the webloggers I know pour their hearts into that page every day they update. Occasionally one of them oversteps (or is perceived to have done so) and a battle begins. It's always about a loss of perspective—and taking oneself too seriously. Approaching your weblog seriously can make it better; taking yourself seriously never will.

RESPONDING TO FLAMES: It is very unlikely, but it may be that you somehow find yourself the subject of an unprovoked attack by another weblogger. If the unfriendly entry is in response to a post that inadvertently gave offense, you may want to email the offended party with your assurance that the post was not intended to give offense. Be very civil in this note; unscrupulous netizens have been known to publish the contents of private chat sessions or email. If the unfriendly entry is really very minor, you may not even want to do this; she may have been having a bad day, and it may be best just to let it pass.

If the unfriendly entry is very vicious, or is clearly unprovoked, just ignore it entirely; there is nothing to be gained by engaging your attacker. Anyone who visits your site in response to these attacks will make their own judgment. Focus on continuing to enjoy maintaining your weblog by expending your energy constructively instead of embroiling yourself in a battle you are unlikely to satisfactorily resolve.

I feel a little silly spending time on this subject. These flame-wars are uncommon and usually pretty minor, and there is no reason to believe you will ever be involved in one. But you should have fair warning that this kind of thing can happen, espe-cially if you are new to the Internet. Just as it takes novices a little while to understand the importance of replacing body language with emoticons when communicating in email, it can take some time to understand how easily a misunderstanding can occur in any online community, and what is an appropriate response.

I have seen many new webloggers, enthusiastic about their new community, confident in their own goodwill, and thor-oughly unfamiliar with participants' histories, jump into weblog controversies when they occur, offering conciliatory, reasoned, or impassioned responses to situations that have their roots in long-standing relationships or patterns of behavior—circumstances of which these newcomers are completely un-aware. A minor controversy becomes a community-wide flamewar only when it spreads from site to site—and usually the situation just needs to be worked out between two people or dropped altogether.

I always feel sorry when I see hapless newcomers leap to the defense of an individual who is known for deliberately stirring up controversy or for attacking those with whom she disagrees. *They'll learn,* I always think. You don't need to. Leave the battle-field to those who love it and concentrate your efforts on con-structive community building.

ASKING FOR A LINK: Every so often I receive an email that says "Hi, please add my weblog to your portal page." Or worse, "Hi, I am interested in trading links with you. Please confirm that you have added me to your site so that I can add you to mine."

What?

Yes, I know that many "experts" will advise you to trade links with others in order to increase traffic to your site, but in the weblog community an email like this is very bad form. Think about it: Almost all of us maintain our weblogs for free, in our spare time. Our only payment is traffic to our sites. More to the point, our reputations are built largely on the quality of the links we provide to our readers, especially in the case of filters. Maintainers of blog-style sites are just as motivated to protect their hard-earned credibility by pointing their readers, when they do link, only to sites that genuinely reflect their taste.

I usually ignore these requests. The notes that demand I add them to my portal always have a bit of an imperious tone to them, which offends me, and sites that threaten not to link to me are just puzzling: I didn't ask.

I was once so irritated upon being approached for a link trade by a new (commercial) site that I actually sent them a rate sheet. The webmaster immediately replied: "Good luck to you and may you go from success to success." It was brilliant. The note made me like him and I felt a bit ashamed for having responded as I did. I still think I was justified in my insistence that if a link on my site was worth asking for, it was worth paying for, but his response taught me how effectively pettiness can be defused by graciousness.

In contrast with telling another weblogger that you admire their work, I think it's iffy to write suggesting that they would enjoy yours. Well, they might, but chances are they already have looked at your weblog if you have linked to them. If they haven't linked you, they might be waiting to see if you make it past the one-month or two-month mark, or they might not have time to make even a small addition to their sidebar.

When I receive a note of this kind, my unwillingness to hurt anyone's feelings is mixed with annoyance that someone has put me in a position to do so, and I know many other webloggers who respond the same way. Putting another weblogger in the awkward position of having to turn you down or ignore your request may make her feel guilty. Since guilt is based on the worry that one is not a good person, your note may make the weblogger whose attention you hope to attract feel vaguely bad about herself. Because none of these feelings originate with her own actions, the weblogger will quickly transform this vaguely bad feeling about herself to a vaguely bad feeling about you. If your goal is to gain allies in the weblog world, putting others in an uncomfortable position is poor strategy.

COMPLAINING ABOUT TRAFFIC: It's equally bad form to complain on your site (or in any public forum) about how little traffic your site receives. Let me say at once that I completely understand this frustration; it happens to everyone. But complaining about it is unattractive. It's very much like the person who walks around complaining that she can never get a date. Hearing her whine incessantly about her unpopularity, many people will wonder why she doesn't engage the group in a topic of general interest, and most of them will be disinclined to invite her to their next party.

You can build awareness of your site with your participation in community activities and by raising your profile in the Internet community at large. Readers will visit your site a second time in response to your unique viewpoint, your writing, and your links. But you will never build a devoted core audience if one of your major themes is the number of people who visit your site every day.

If there is one guiding principle in all of these admonitions it might be: Avoid histrionics. Complaining about other webloggers, engaging in infighting, whining about traffic, and demanding that others pay you your due will eventually make you unpopular with the community and alienate your readers.

Weblog Etiquette

CREDITING LINKS: Perhaps the longest-standing piece of weblog etiquette is crediting links found via another weblog. I think this evolved partially from the glee with which the earliest weblogs found other sites like theirs. But there were a couple of other important considerations as well.

Remember that the early weblogs were filters. These weblog editors earned their reputations based on the quality of the links they published. In that light, grabbing a link from another weblog without mentioning where it was found is dishonest—and would have been widely perceived as an attempt to build a reputation on someone else's hard work. This scrupulous sense of honor was reinforced by the small size of the community. When there were fewer than thirty sites to read, all of the webloggers read all of the weblogs. It was obvious to the entire community when an individual lifted links without giving credit.

A few webloggers don't bother with this common courtesy, but I think it's a very important tradition. When you are new, it is a respectful way to announce your presence to the weblog community. Once you have gained an audience, it is a service to your readers, who will be pleased by a pointer to another site that discusses the subjects they are interested in. And once you have built a steady core audience, it's a gracious way to introduce lesser known weblogs to your readers and to others in your weblog cluster.

While the weblog universe is immense, individual clusters are still small enough that if you choose not to credit your links, the omission will be noted. You may not feel that this custom is particularly valuable, but you should realize that even the most conscientious link creditor might feel disinclined to credit a weblog that never extends the same courtesy to others.

New webloggers often wonder how far back to trace a credit. You have found a great link on weblog A, which credits weblog B, which credits weblog C. Should you mention them all? The convention is to credit only one generation back. Interested readers can take the journey back link by link if they are really interested in tracking the meme.

What if you find the link on one weblog, make a note to add it to your weblog, and then see it on another? Do you credit them both, or try to determine which of them posted the link first? When a link is very widespread, weblogs often credit "found almost everywhere." Otherwise, I usually credit the weblog that brought the link to my attention, reasoning, I suppose, that I could have stopped surfing as soon as I found it. Similarly, if you find a link on your own, make a note of it, and then happen to find it linked on another weblog, there's no real reason to credit the link, since you didn't find it there.

ANNOUNCING YOUR SCHEDULE: It's certainly not necessary, but many webloggers make a short announcement just before taking time off for vacation or when embarking on a project that will prevent them from updating their site. This is a courtesy to their readers who otherwise would continue visiting every day to see if something new has been posted. You needn't feel that you should announce if you are going to miss one day or even a few, but if you know in advance that your schedule is going to change, why not announce it publicly so that your readers can plan to resume their regular visits when updates begin again? Additionally, when an active site suddenly goes silent, readers worry. If you begin receiving email asking if you are all right, do the rest of your readers the kindness of announcing that you are taking a break.

When I began writing this book, I put a short note on my site: "Heads Up: I'm starting a big project, so I'm going to aim to update the Pocket Monday, Wednesday, and Friday." That was it. But it told my readers what to expect, and it freed me to spend the time I needed on the rest of my life without having to juggle too many balls or feel guilty for letting a few of them drop.

If you need to miss updating your site for just a day or two, it really is no big deal, and you should never feel obligated to apologize. An involving offline life may leave you less time for your weblog, but as a rule, a balanced person is a more interesting writer. If you know you will be gone for a week or more, or if you plan to change your regular schedule, it is a courtesy to your readers to let them know.

GIVING FAIR WARNING: Always warn your readers when you link to a document or file they may regret clicking. This can range from a disturbing news story or photograph, to nudity or other potentially offensive material. Readers may also wish to avoid pages that include embedded music, spawn pop-up windows, or contain so many graphics that they will take a long time to download.

When linking to anything that is not an HTML file (e.g., Flash, PDF, Word) let your readers know so that they can decide whether they want to click through. When linking to audio or video files, make a note of the format (e.g., RealAudio, QuickTime, Windows Media). Multimedia files can be very large and can take a very long time to download over a modem. Additionally, some file types and media formats are incompatible with certain operating systems, or may lock up older computers. Others will insist on installing a plug-in, which many people find annoying. Let your readers decide before they click.

When linking to a site that requires free registration, state that fact alongside the link. Similarly, if you decide to link a story from a site that requires a paid subscription, make a note of it, but understand that few of your readers are likely to click through.

ANSWERING EMAIL: I know of one very popular weblogger who is revered for his policy of answering every note he receives. Because other webloggers and I read his site, know that he works, witness his wide involvement in the online community, and yet always receive at least a brief response whenever we write, we all suspect that he doesn't often sleep or sleeps only a few hours every night.

I know of another weblogger who never answers his email, or at least not the email I send. Occasionally even this individual is impelled to post a note on his weblog saying that he simply does not have the time to answer messages, vaguely implying that his vast, talky audience would leave him time for little else if he did.

Most of us fall into a middle ground. I want to answer all of my email, and I really mean to do so one day. Occasionally I will take a weekend day to go through my inbox, starting with the oldest notes first and working my way to more recent dates as time permits. One Saturday in November I made my way through the entire month of September, but then the next weekend I was too busy to look at my email at all. It's very strange because I don't feel like I receive an inordinate amount of reader correspondence, and yet when I look at my inbox it always seems to be full, and too many of the notes have been there an embarrassing length of time.

If you are maintaining a professional site, you probably will automatically answer every note, but if you are maintaining a personal site and for any reason you don't want to answer email, just don't do it and don't apologize. You may want to omit your email address from your site or place a note on your site saying that you generally do not reply to the notes you receive. You are doing your site in your spare time, and no one can reasonably fault you for placing limits on the amount of time and type of effort you want to expend on your hobby.

For the rest of us, I can only advise what I have not yet successfully managed: Schedule an hour or two every week devoted to answering your reader email or religiously answer every note with a cordial one-sentence reply when it comes in. I don't think this is usually an issue for new webloggers, who are often desperate for any feedback and thrilled to discover that anyone at all reads their site. But if your audience grows and you really do receive an unmanageable amount of reader email, you might consider adding a comment system to your site in the hope of funneling off some of that feedback into a forum that doesn't necessarily require a response. Otherwise, I think a systematic approach is the only effective means of keeping your inbox from becoming cluttered with reader mail.

Weblog Ethics

Weblogs are the mavericks of the online world. Two of their greatest strengths are their ability to filter and disseminate information to a widely dispersed audience, and their position outside the mainstream of mass media. Beholden to no one, weblogs point to, comment on, and spread information according to their own, quirky criteria.

The weblog network's potential influence may be the real reason mainstream news organizations have begun investigating the phenomenon, and it probably underlies much of the talk about weblogs as journalism. Webloggers may not think in terms of control and influence, but commercial media do. Mass media seeks, above all, to gain a wide audience. Advertising revenues, the lifeblood of any professional publication or broadcast, depend on the size of that publication's audience. Content, from a business standpoint, is there only to deliver eyeballs to advertisers, whether the medium is paper or television.

Journalists—the people who actually report the news—are acutely aware of the potential for abuse that is inherent in their system, which relies on support from businesses and power brokers, each with an agenda to promote. Their ethical standards are designed to delineate the journalist's responsibilities and provide a clear code of conduct that will ensure the integrity of the news.

Weblogs, produced by nonprofessionals, have no such code, and individual webloggers seem almost proud of their amateur status. "We don't need no stinkin' fact checkers" seems to be the prevailing attitude, as if inaccuracy were a virtue.

Let me propose a radical notion: The weblog's greatest strength—its uncensored, unmediated, uncontrolled voice—is also its greatest weakness. News outlets may be ultimately beholden to advertising interests, and reporters may have a strong incentive for remaining on good terms with their sources in order to remain in the loop; but because they are businesses with salaries to pay, advertisers to please, and audiences to attract and hold, professional news organizations have a vested interest in upholding certain standards so that readers keep subscribing and advertisers keep buying. Weblogs, with only minor costs and little hope of significant financial gain, have no such incentives.

The very things that may compromise professional news outlets are at the same time incentives for some level of journalistic standards. And the very things that make weblogs so valuable as alternative news sources—the lack of gatekeepers and the freedom from all consequences—may compromise their integrity and thus their value. There is every indication that weblogs will gain even greater influence as their numbers grow and awareness of the form becomes more widespread. It is not true, as some people assert, that the network will route around misinformation, or that the truth is always filtered to widespread awareness. Rumors spread because they are fun to pass along. Corrections rarely gain much traction either in the real world or online; they just aren't as much fun.

There has been almost no talk about ethics in the weblog universe: Mavericks are notoriously resistant to being told what to do. But I would propose a set of six rules that I think form a basis of ethical behavior for online publishers of all kinds.[1] I hope that the weblog community will thoughtfully consider the principles outlined here; in time, and with experience, the community may see the need to add to these rules or to further codify our standards. At the very least, I hope these principles will spur discussion about our responsibilities and the ramifications of our collective behavior.

Journalistic codes of ethics seek to ensure fairness and accuracy in news reporting. By comparison, each of these suggestions attempts to bring transparency—one of the weblog's distinguishing characteristics and greatest strengths—into every aspect of the practice of weblogging. It is unrealistic to expect every weblogger to present an even-handed picture of the world, but it is very reasonable to expect them to be forthcoming about their sources, biases, and behavior.

Webloggers who, despite my best efforts, persist in their quest to be regarded as journalists will have a special interest in adhering to these principles. News organizations may someday be willing to point to weblogs (or weblog entries) as serious sources, but only if weblogs have, as a whole, demonstrated integrity in their information gathering and dissemination, and consistency in their online conduct.

Any weblogger who expects to be accorded the privileges and protections of a professional journalist will need to go further than these principles. Rights have associated responsibilities; in

---

[1]With regard to points 1 and 5, I am indebted to Dave Winer for his discussions on Scripting News about integrity with regard to weblogging. Though our thinking diverges greatly, his ideas were one springboard for my own thoughts on the matter. http://scriptingnews.userland.com/backissues/2002/02/04#integrity

the end it is an individual's professionalism and meticulous observance of recognized ethical standards that determines her status in the eyes of society and the law. For the rest of us, I believe the following standards are sufficient:

1. Publish as fact only that which you believe to be true.

If your statement is speculation, say so. If you have reason to believe that something is not true, either don't post it, or note your reservations. When you make an assertion, do so in good faith; state it as fact only if, to the best of your knowledge, it is so.

2. If material exists online, link to it when you reference it.

Linking to referenced material allows readers to judge for themselves the accuracy and insightfulness of your statements. Referencing material but selectively linking only that with which you agree is manipulative. Online readers deserve, as much as possible, access to all of the facts—the Web, used this way, empowers readers to become active, not passive, consumers of information. Further, linking to source material is the very means by which we are creating a vast, new, collective network of information and knowledge.

On the rare occasion when a writer wishes to reference but not drive traffic to a site she considers to be morally reprehensible (for example, a hate site), she should type out (but not link) the name or URL of the offending site and state the reasons for her decision. This will give motivated readers the information they need to find the site in order to make their own judgment. This strategy allows the writer to preserve her own transparency (and thus her integrity) while simultaneously declining to lend support to a cause she finds contemptible.

3. Publicly correct any misinformation.

If you find that you have linked to a story that was untrue, make a note of it and link to a more accurate report. If one of your own statements proves to be inaccurate, note your misstatement and the truth. Ideally, these corrections would appear in the most current version of your weblog and as an added note to the original entry. (Remember that search engines will pull up entries without regard to when they were posted; once an entry exists in your archives, it may continue to spread an untruth even if you corrected the information a few days later.) If you aren't willing to add a correction to previous entries, at least note it in a later post.

One clear method of denoting a correction is the one employed by Cory Doctorow, one of the contributors to the Boing Boing weblog. He strikes through any erroneous information and adds the corrected information immediately following. The reader can see at a glance what ~~Bill~~ Cory originally wrote and that he has updated the entry with information he feels to be more accurate. (Do it like this in HTML: The reader can see at a glance what <strike>Bill</strike> Cory originally wrote and that he has updated the entry with information he feels to be more accurate.)

4. Write each entry as if it could not be changed; add to, but do not rewrite or delete, any entry.

Post deliberately. If you invest each entry with intent, you will ensure your personal and professional integrity.

Changing or deleting entries destroys the integrity of the network. The Web is designed to be connected; indeed, the weblog permalink is an invitation for others to link. Anyone who comments on or cites a document on the Web relies on that document (or entry) to remain unchanged. A prominent addendum is the preferred way to correct any information anywhere on the Web. If an addendum is impractical, as in the case of an essay that contains numerous inaccuracies, changes must be noted with the date and a brief description of the nature of the change.

If you think this is overly scrupulous, consider the case of the writer who points to an online document in support of an assertion. If this document changes or disappears—and especially if the change is not noted—her argument may be rendered nonsensical. Books do not change; journals are static. On paper, new versions are always denoted as such.

The network of shared knowledge we are building will never be more than a novelty unless we protect its integrity by creating permanent records of our publications. The network benefits when even entries that are rendered irrelevant by changing circumstance are left as a historical record. As an example: A weblogger complains about inaccuracies in an online article; the writer corrects those inaccuracies (and notes them!); the weblogger's entry is therefore meaningless—or is it? Deleting the entry somehow asserts that the whole incident simply didn't happen—but it did. The record is more accurate and history is better served if the weblogger notes beneath the original entry that the writer has made the corrections and the article is now, to the weblogger's knowledge, accurate.

History can be rewritten, but it cannot be undone. Changing or deleting words is possible on the Web, but possibility does not always make good policy. Think before you publish and stand behind what you write. If you later decide you were wrong about something, make a note of it and move on.

I make a point never to post anything I am not willing to stand behind even if I later disagree. I work to be thoughtful and accurate, no matter how angry or excited I am about a particular topic. If I change my opinion in a day or two, I just note the change. If I need to apologize for something I've said, I do so.

If you discover that you have posted erroneous information, you *must* note this publicly on your weblog. Deleting the offending entry will do nothing to correct the misinformation your readers have already absorbed. Taking the additional step of adding a correction to the original entry will ensure that Google broadcasts accurate information into the future.

The only exception to this rule is when you inadvertently reveal personal information about someone else. If you discover that you have violated a confidence or made an acquaintance uncomfortable by mentioning him, it is only fair to remove the offending entry altogether, but note that you have done so.

5. Disclose any conflict of interest.

Most webloggers are quite transparent about their jobs and professional interests. It is the computer programmer's expertise that gives her commentary special weight when she analyzes a magazine article about the merits of the latest operating system. Since weblog audiences are built on trust, it is to every weblogger's benefit to disclose any monetary (or other potentially conflicting) interests when appropriate. An entrepreneur may have special insight into the effect of a proposed Senate bill or a business merger; if she stands to benefit directly from the outcome of any event, she should note that in her comments. A weblogger, impressed with a service or product, should note that she holds stock in the company every time she promotes the service on her page. Even the weblogger who receives a CD for review should note that fact; her readers can decide for themselves whether her favorable review is based on her taste or on her desire to continue to receive free CDs.

Quickly note any potential conflict of interest and then say your piece; your readers will have all the information they need to assess your commentary.

6. Note questionable and biased sources.

When a serious article comes from a highly biased or questionable source, the weblogger has a responsibility to clearly note the nature of the site on which it was found.

In their foraging, webloggers occasionally find interesting, well-written articles on sites that are maintained by highly biased organizations or by seemingly fanatical individuals. Readers need to know whether an article on the medical ramifications of first trimester abortion comes from a site that is pro-life, pro-choice, or strongly opposed to medical intervention of all kinds. A thoughtful summation of the Israeli-Palestinian conflict may be worth reading whether it is written by a member of the PLO or a Zionist—but readers have the right to be alerted to the source.

It is reasonable to expect that expert foragers have the knowledge and motivation to assess the nature of these sources; it is not reasonable to assume that all readers do. Readers depend on weblogs, to some extent, for guidance in navigating the Web. To present an article from a source that is a little nutty or has a strong agenda is fine; not to acknowledge the nature of that source is unethical, since readers don't have the information they need to fully evaluate the article's merits.

If you are afraid that your readers will discount the article entirely based on its context, consider why you are linking it at all. If you strongly feel the piece has merit, say why and let it stand on its own, but be clear about its source. Your readers may cease to trust you if they discover even once that you disguised—or didn't make clear—the source of an article they might have evaluated differently had they been given all the facts.

Gaining Credibility

You gain credibility in the weblog community and with the weblog-reading public in exactly the same way you do in any other arena: by your conscientiousness and hard work. The best thing you can do to gain readers is to provide them with interesting, varied content. No matter what kind of site you maintain, readers will return when they find something on your site that they won't find anywhere else.

If you are maintaining a subject-specific weblog, this means searching all the usual sources for information pertaining to your field and then carefully sorting through the results for articles that are fresh, informative, and valuable. It means exploring unlikely avenues to find the stories that may not obviously pertain to your field but that, to your expert eye, are of great relevance. If you maintain a general-interest filter, it means trying new writing styles, exploring different sources. It means finding an important or interesting article and then reading numerous other sources for the one that tells the story best. It means digging up background information or earlier articles to provide context for the articles you link and expressing your opinions as clearly and concisely as you can.

If you are maintaining a notebook or blog, it means paying particular attention to your writing and being constantly on the lookout for engaging subject matter. It means courageously choosing to write honestly about the things you choose to share, and pushing yourself just a little way out of your comfort zone when you relate your experiences to your readers. It means paying attention to details, like commas, and spelling—and the color of her eyes. It means reading deeply and well, and learning how to tell a story. It means coming to the page regularly.

Why bother seeking credibility with the weblog community? Even if you became interested in creating your own weblog because you saw untapped possibilities in the form, it's likely that your interest was ignited by reading the work of one or a few writers. Like you, most weblog writers are weblog fans. And though none of us can hope to be read by every other weblogger, the Weblog Nation potentially can be a built-in base of readers. When other weblogs pick up one of your links or point their readers to an entry, their respect for your work is lever-

Item: 31267420018663
Title: Crazy sexy diet : eat your veggi
es, ignite your spark, and live like you m
ean it!
Call no.: 613.262 C
Due: 5/5/2011

Item: 31267137069793
Title: The weblog handbook : practical
advice on creating and maintaining your bl
og
Call no.: 005.72 B
Due: 5/5/2011

Total Items: 4

Howard County Library delivers high-
quality public education for all ages.

aged and your weblog gains exposure to ten or twenty or one hundred new pairs of eyes.

Another reason is the common desire to be respected by those you respect. It's very gratifying to find a link to your site on the page of a weblogger you feel does consistently excellent work. The qualities that engage your general audience will gain you the respect of other webloggers, who are, after all, merely converted weblog fans. More than the rest of your audience, other webloggers are in a position to see just what it takes to do what you do, and your depth and breadth will resonate with them even more strongly than with your other readers.

Finally, I know from my own experience how gratifying it is to belong to a community, even one as far-flung and diffuse as this one has become. Finding an email in my inbox containing a comment on one of my articles (and maybe a link!) or a note simply wishing me a happy holiday season reminds me that I am engaged with a group of people who value the same things I do: strong opinions, vigorous self-expression, and a desire to share our vision with the world. I have been fortunate to meet face to face with various groups of webloggers and I have found them to be, without exception, genuinely nice individuals. Several of these have been webloggers with whom, politically, I could not disagree more strongly (and I know that I appear equally wrong-headed to them). In each case we have met each other with great pleasure, our differences far, far outweighed by the things we have in common: a love for the weblog, the unwavering belief in the value of every individual's opinion, and an absolute commitment to the right of each of us to publish our thoughts.

Using Your Powers for Good

If I were King, no one in my realm would go hungry, war would not be tolerated, and everyone would have a sturdy house, affordable health care, and a good education.

Alas, I am but a lowly weblogger, yet on my site visitors can click a link to donate food for free, support Doctors Without Borders, or make a donation to the Heifer Project. As part of Link and Think I provide my readers with information on HIV/AIDS every December 1 in observance of World AIDS Day. Even if my site is read by only five or ten of my closest friends, I know I make a difference by pointing to solutions as often as I point to problems, and I try to make it easy for all of my readers to do good.

I have made it a personal policy to occasionally highlight lesser-known weblogs on my site, and I have been very pleased to see a few of them become well known, at least in certain weblog clusters. A word from me does not ensure popularity by any measure, but readers who enjoy my weblog may be inclined to click through to another one that I recommend.

I take real pleasure when, in my daily rounds, I see a "via" link to a site I highlighted the day or two before, especially when I feel that the two weblogs are particularly suited to each other. It's like introducing two people at a party, certain that they will hit it off, and then seeing that they have. I know that I can't bring another weblog an audience, but by occasionally mentioning another weblog I can, perhaps, give someone else a hand up. Even if you feel that your audience is quite small, I heartily encourage you to do the same.

I even send other webloggers links I think they may be interested in. Often something is of mild interest to me, but it seems to be exactly in the range for someone else. I know that they may not link it, and I am never offended if they do not. But I enjoy sharing information (why else would I have a weblog?) and if it might be useful to someone else, I'm glad to pass it along.

I know that some weblog writers consider gaining a weblog audience to be a zero-sum game: that every person who reads my weblog is less likely to read theirs. I don't agree. I see weblogs as the online equivalent of salted peanuts—it's impossible to stop snacking after eating only one—and I think that every reader I gain is likely sooner or later to go on the prowl for other sites like mine. I am convinced that every new reader of any weblog benefits all of us and that what strengthens one in the community strengthens us all.

I am not the King, and yet I have the ability to educate a diverse group of people about causes and charitable organizations that I think deserve wider support. On my weblog I can point to other independent publishers with open respect. I can scrupulously give credit where credit is due, and I can refuse to drive traffic to any person I feel is doing harm in the community. On my weblog I have complete power to reward the worthy, ignore the ignoble, fight tirelessly for what is right, and speak for those who cannot speak for themselves. It's my weblog, and it's good to be King.

Referenced Weblogs

Boing Boing	http://boingboing.net/

Journalism Codes of Ethics

Society of Professional Journalists Code of Ethics	http://www.spj.org/ethics_code.asp
The Poynter High School Journalism Guide Ethics Checklist	http://www.poynter.org/centerpiece/highschool/ethics_checklist.htm
Guiding Principles for Journalists	http://www.poynter.org/dj/tips/ethics/me_gdeho.htm
International Journalists Network—International Codes of Ethics	http://www.ijnet.org/code.html
European Codes of Journalism Ethics	http://www.uta.fi/ethicnet/

7

Living Online

We've all heard that the unexamined life is not worth living, but consider too that the unlived life is not worth examining.

JULIA CAMERON

The great myth about keeping a weblog is that suddenly every detail of one's life is published for public consumption. Only a moment's thought will reveal the foolishness of such a view: Every weblogger decides what to publish and what to withhold. Or to put it another way, sharing the details of your life requires a deliberate effort; keeping them private requires none at all. But some aspects of creating an online presence are not obvious to the newcomer, or at least were not always obvious to me. What follows are a few observations on the day-to-day business of maintaining a weblog.

Creating a Schedule

Most weblogs are unfunded, spare-time ventures, yet most webloggers update their sites five days a week, and some even work on weekends! It's true that the only way to cultivate an audience is to provide them with new content on a regular basis. Becoming a slave to your weblog schedule is a sure way to burn out, so the first thing I advise you to do is to create a reasonable schedule for yourself and then to stick to it. If you are maintaining a work-related weblog, you have two choices: schedule a few hours every workday for surfing and writing, or just add entries as you find information throughout the day.

Your choice should be determined by your online habits and your work schedule. If your work is mostly self-directed and you find yourself taking frequent breaks, updating throughout the day may be the least disruptive schedule. If you must be away from your desk much of the day, or if your work requires long stretches of uninterrupted time, you will probably find that you work best if you can schedule a block of time that will not interfere with or be interfered by your other work. However, if your weblog is a personal venture, you will need to make another plan.

It is an open secret that some people surf the Web while they are at work. It may be less well known that some webloggers update their weblogs from work. This was very common in those halcyon early days, when dot-coms hired young coders for low pay and the promise of large stock options, fed them substantial quantities of sugar, and kept them at work for sixteen hours a day—nearly all of their waking hours.

I don't advise you to update your weblog from work. Leaving aside the question of ethics, many companies now use "spyware" designed to log every keystroke of every employee across the company. Whether or not your company has implemented such software, time you spend updating your weblog is bound to affect your work performance, and no pastime is worth losing your next promotion or even your job. If you are self-employed, you may find strict adherence to this rule even more valuable, since there will be no one to pick up the slack when you waste precious work hours composing entries about the filtering mechanism on your coffeemaker.

I have never updated my weblog from work (really!), so for me weblogging has always been a spare-time activity. I typically need a couple of hours to update my site. I spend that time surfing the Web, evaluating any URLs that I may have collected during the day and writing individual entries. Sometimes I spend some time searching for another version of a news story or hunting for additional information about a particular event. Once I've written my linktext, I spend a little time arranging the entries on the page.

The schedule you set for yourself should closely resemble the one you already keep. If you typically spend an hour every morning surfing the Web, this is the time you should use to update your weblog. If you read online every night after the kids are in bed, this will be your weblogging time. Your spouse or significant other has adjusted to this schedule and is presumably already using the time to write a children's book or construct a model of the Battle of Antioch. If you already spend several hours a day online, I doubt that maintaining your weblog will add to it substantially; but you may feel that the time you spend is more focused and ultimately better spent.

Online Reputation . . . Again

As I have said before, everything you do online creates your reputation, and this reputation is defined only by the words you publish. Nothing you do in real life follows you onto the page. None of your physical mannerisms, habits, or actions affect the way you are perceived on a mailing list, discussion board, or website. The courtesy you show in always allowing others to finish their sentences before you respond; the kindness with which you regard children when you pass them on the street; the respect you demonstrate by always offering your seat to the elderly; your generosity in tipping—none of this shows online. Only your words do, and your silence.

Another major difference between the Internet and real life is that everything you say online may live forever. Think about that for a moment.

How would you feel if anyone could walk into the employee lounge, speak your name, and have everything you ever said in that room replayed for them? What if anyone who cared to could witness the tantrum you (uncharacteristically) threw on the day when a crucial sales presentation was due, your computer's hard drive crashed, tech support was nowhere to be found, and after an hour of searching frantically for help you found the network guy next to the coffeemaker flirting with the cute bicycle messenger? Or the tart, personally dismissive remark (or worse) you made one morning to the driver who cut you off on the way to an important final exam that had started five minutes before? And what if, even when those actions were followed by an effusive apology, there was no guarantee that either the context of your remarks or the apology that followed would ever be seen in conjunction with the events?

On the Internet, mailing lists may be archived (officially or unofficially by list members), and websites may be cached (by Google or in someone's browser) or archived (by you or by projects such as the Internet Archive, whose mission is to create a historical record of the Web). A webpage can be captured as an image and posted on another website, providing a snapshot of any given moment for all posterity, or as evidence that you published something that you later removed. Once you become active in the online community, whether by maintaining a website, participating in mailing lists, or posting in any online discussion group, a quick search for your name on Google will likely result in an informative history of your life online: a selection of your best and worst moments, and others' reactions to you, arranged arbitrarily, with no context provided.

Remember, too, that your online reputation can have real-life ramifications. Web-savvy employers faced with a high stack of resumes may search Google to see what they can find. If your online presence is consistently belligerent, they may elect to interview a different candidate. This isn't paranoid fantasy. One weblogger recently lost her job after complaining vociferously on her weblog about her place of work.

So perhaps the most important bit of advice contained in this book is: Choose your topics with deliberation. Think before you publish anything online. When I say publish, I mean a post to your weblog, an email to a mailing list or another weblogger, a message on a discussion board, or an essay on your site.

I am not proposing that you become a milquetoast or that you never express a strong opinion. Indeed, I believe that your weblog is interesting in direct proportion to the strength of your passion, and the frequency with which you share that on your page. Passion is the purpose of the weblog: passion for a profession or hobby, passion for telling stories, passion for punditry, even a passion for civil, well-reasoned debate. The things you are sure about, the things you can't figure out, and the things you find interesting—all are colored by the extent to which you care; if you don't care, you might as well not publish at all.

When you are composing a post, whether it be on your weblog, on a mailing list, on a discussion board, or in private email to another weblogger, there are two situations in which you will want to exercise extreme restraint.

Each of us has bad days, and each of us has been acquainted with someone who simply rubs us the wrong way. When writing in either of these situations, you would be well advised not to publish at all. If you find yourself becoming very angry when composing an email, a personal entry to your weblog, or a post to a discussion board, stop and save the post into a text editor, then put it away for the moment. If after twenty minutes you can't stop thinking about the subject, by all means go back into your text editor and type to your heart's content.

After you've composed your message, go back through and edit out all of the personal attacks, specious arguments, and unsupported claims. Once that is done, edit it again, this time with the goal of removing any inflammatory language and replacing it with a more neutral representation of your point of view. When you have reworked your message to your satisfaction, show it to a trusted friend and rework your message until *they* feel your note clearly states your point of view in clear, noninflammatory language.

If at any time during this process you become bored, put the note away. If at any time during this process you lose interest in responding, put the note away. If, after doing all this work you still want to publish your note, go ahead. But do not ever post a note you have written in anger. It is unlikely to make your point convincingly, and it probably will create general bad feeling or potentially even an enemy—and all of those things will damage your reputation.

The other situation in which you should use extreme caution is when you want to comment on a topic likely to be controversial. First, decide whether you really want to comment on the topic at all. If your comments are certain to stir up bad feeling, you may want to remain silent rather than engage in an emotional debate or become the object of attacks by others. The world will not cease revolving around the sun if you do not weigh in on a particular subject, and if there is little likelihood of ever getting your point across or even coming to a compromise position, it may be best simply to remain silent.

Many respected webloggers seem to make it their policy never to engage in a debate about controversial subjects (especially those that concern the weblog community itself); only they know whether this reflects their utter lack of interest in the topic or in the practice of online debate. I can pretty much guarantee that your readers who do not maintain weblogs simply could not care less about any controversy about the weblog community itself. In fact, many of your weblog-writing readers are equally uninterested. When the controversy revolves around the weblog community itself, the wisest course usually is to quietly refuse to become embroiled in the debate-du-jour and allow those who enjoy the fray to have the field.

Even when responding to the comments another weblogger has made on a more substantial topic, always strive for extreme clarity. A subject is controversial only because people's responses to it are so very emotional. Many people are not able to put aside their emotions long enough to genuinely understand a differing point of view, and, in my experience, most are not willing even to try. When you link to another weblogger's remarks on a subject, you engage him in a public conversation; make it a rule to do so only with the utmost respect.

Because you are publicly stating that you disagree, take extra care to write in a clear, noncontentious manner. You are striving to express your views to those able to listen, while not handing the irrational opposition anything to sink their teeth into. Strip your comments of personal attacks and statements that are not grounded in fact. Either of these will give an opponent ample opportunity to discredit you without having to address the substance of your argument. If your fellow weblogger responds by attacking you, simply drop the subject and make a note not to engage him again.

I am not suggesting that you publish only watered-down opinions about safe subjects. Quite the opposite: Your weblog will be most interesting when you speak fearlessly about the things you feel most strongly about. I am counseling you to avoid embroiling yourself in controversies you care little about, and to always approach your colleagues with respect. Most of all, I am advising you to write so that you will be willing to stand behind everything you publish on the Internet, even if you disagree with it in a few years. You will never need to be ashamed of anything you have written if you are always respectful of others and their opinions, and if your thoughts are well reasoned and carefully expressed.

Maintaining Your Privacy

As I said at the beginning of this chapter, your weblog is revealing only to the extent that you make it so. But as I have noted, life online is more permanent than life on the street, and today's offhand remark may live forever in a mailing list archive, or on someone else's hard drive.

When I started writing online, I decided to publish only the most oblique references to my personal life. For one thing, my personal life isn't particularly interesting, and for another, I like keeping private things private. I have not been shy in expressing my opinions and I've always felt that anyone could read my weblog or explore my site and come out with a pretty detailed picture of my interests and opinions. As time has passed, little bits of information about my life have been posted now and again, but I focus my weblog on the ideas I find interesting, not on myself.

On finding one of my essays linked on a new (to me) weblog, I was a little dismayed to read a couple of references to some recent events in my life that would have taken some digging around to put together. "I'm not stalking her," the weblogger went on to say. "Rebecca has an extensive site and it's all right there." Well, I guess it is. But not on the top page and not in one place. I was flattered that anyone had liked my writing well enough to so thoroughly explore my site, but, knowing how far apart those two pieces of information resided, it was disconcerting to think of anyone poking around so very meticulously through my past offhand remarks.

The only point to this story is that you should never post anything on your weblog that you are not comfortable having published out in the world. If you maintain archives, every little personal reference will be easily accessible to the interested public. When you write about a personal subject, remember that it will not be spoken once and then fade away. If this makes you feel the least bit uncomfortable about posting a particular entry or link, don't do it! There are other (possibly more interesting) things to write about.

Maintain whatever level of privacy is most comfortable for you. I know one weblogger who publishes her address online and I know of another who has managed to obscure even their gender. Just remember that you are under no obligation to provide the weblog-reading public with even an iota of information about yourself. You do them the favor of updating your site on a regular basis, and you owe them nothing more.

Protecting the Privacy of Others

Whatever your comfort level with making personal revelations, I feel that everyone publishing online should be respectful of other people's privacy. Putting the details of your own life online is one thing; publishing the details of someone else's life is quite another. It is never acceptable to publish a transcript of an instant message, chat-room conversation, or email on your weblog without the express permission of all of the participants. This seems ridiculously obvious, but I have seen each of these things published on websites without the permission of the sender. Don't do it.

The same rule applies to real-life conversations. No one enjoys visiting a page only to discover snippets of their real life published for the world to see. Few people will object if you recount a particularly witty bit of repartee. But don't go have coffee with friends and then come home and publish their snippy opinions about your mutual acquaintances.

In general, it is a terrible idea ever to meet with an acquaintance and then report the entire conversation on your weblog. This holds true for meetings with webloggers as well as civilians. Doing this even once is likely to reduce both the availability of your friends and the quality of conversation you have with the acquaintances you have left, since everyone you know will be constantly editing themselves for publication on your website. If you think of seven interesting things while talking to someone, write about them. But unless someone else's comment is completely nonpersonal, leave it off your page. No one you know should ever feel the need to say, "Don't post this on your weblog." If you ever do hear those words, you may need to reevaluate your posting habits.

On the other hand, if you are in the habit of posting the smart and witty observations of others without attribution, you may garner resentment among your friends and colleagues. Just as it is rude in everyday life to take credit for another person's ideas, it is rude to do it on the page. "Sharyn made an interesting observation about jackhammers yesterday . . ." is a polite way to both entertain your audience and give credit where credit is due.

Of course you will never repeat any confidence on your website, even with all identities obscured. How horrible. When someone reveals to you a very personal story, they do so with the understanding that you will honor their privacy. If you want to write about intensely personal matters, dig into your own psyche, but leave others out of it.

These are the same commonsense rules that you use in making everyday decisions about what to reveal to others about your acquaintances, with the additional caveat that an offhand remark online will not disappear after it is made. If you discover after the fact that your acquaintances are uncomfortable having either their words or their name published on your page, remove it. In your everyday life, if you discover that Sharyn considers her relationship with jackhammers to be a very personal matter, you can refrain from repeating her observations in the future. Online, you must remove the remark or her name in order to prevent either from being repeated every time someone looks at the page. (If you remove the remark, briefly note the removal in case anyone has pointed to it.)

If you are in the habit of writing about your everyday life, you may find it very awkward to completely expunge your friends from your accounts. If you need to refer to your acquaintances, use first names only, or initials if that is more comfortable. When stories often revolve around a recurring cast of characters, some webloggers have chosen to apply pseudonyms: "SO" for significant other, or "the Drama Queen" for an acquaintance with an emotionally complicated life. In general, use your common sense and respect others' limits when you write about them.

Protecting Children

It is wise to take the same precautions to protect your children online as you do in everyday life. Numerous webloggers and journalers routinely refer to their children by name and even post an occasional picture. Likely, this is as safe as milk. But I would caution you to think carefully about publishing information that could tie your children to a physical location: the name of their school, your home address, or even a teacher's name, if your website makes clear what city you live in. Remember that your online activity creates a searchable repository of personal factoids, and do what you must to protect your child's identity accordingly.

If a child is under your personal protection, you should make decisions based on your own circumstances and comfort level; but any child who is living with someone else must be protected to the utmost of your ability. If you post a picture of your family, identify everyone by first name only, or not at all. Ensure that no photographs can be tied to a physical location by an address in the background or even a very distinctive piece of architecture.

If you post a piece of artwork, identify the youngster by first name only, or, if the name is very unusual, by a more obscure reference ("a six-year-old acquaintance" or "my friend's daughter"). Never mention the name of the children's school if you have referenced them by name or posted a picture. Since you are not there to protect them, you must make it impossible for anyone to use your website to trace any child to a physical location.

If your weblog is devoted to keeping your friends and relatives up-to-date on the daily details of your family life, consider making it private. Some Web hosts allow you to password-protect your site (and usually provide you with directions on how to do so). This will require your family members to log in each time they want to read your weblog, but it will prevent casual surfers from poking around your site. Some weblog management tools automatically generate a listing of newly updated sites that use their service; your service should allow you to designate your weblog as "public" (meaning that it will appear on that list) or "private" (meaning that it will not).

If you want your site to be private but you cannot prevent your weblog management tool from publishing your URL to a public list, choose another tool. Practically speaking, if your URL is not published anywhere, no one will visit your site. Keeping yourself off public weblog listings, asking your family not to pass your URL to others, and refraining from linking to other sites should provide your family weblog with a reasonable level of privacy. The Web is a friendly place with a few weirdos, just like your hometown. Understand what it means to be online and make appropriate decisions for yourself and your family.

Webcams and Photos

Some webloggers maintain webcams (a little camera mounted to a computer that broadcasts a video image to the Web), and many include a photograph of themselves somewhere on their site. Again, this is a matter of personal comfort. Your photograph will remove yet another layer between your online persona and your everyday life; indeed, this is exactly why so many webloggers feel compelled to publish photographs of themselves in the first place. Many are extremely comfortable expanding their offline lives into their online existence; for them, the Internet is merely an extension of their physical environment. Others include their photograph as a design element on their page, as part of their header. Some people seek only to add a small personal touch to an otherwise barren expanse of words.

If you are not comfortable publishing your picture online, don't do it. Be aware that many webloggers are inveterate documentarians, so if you attend a face-to-face gathering, make a point of letting those with cameras know that you would like to be excluded from any photographs that will be posted on the Web. If you are one of the photographers, it is extra polite to email those whose pictures you plan to publish in order to get their permission to do so.

If you elect to publish your photograph (or allow others to publish it), be aware that there is a small chance you will be recognized when you are at the supermarket. It sounds ridiculous, but I know of people who have been recognized in public by readers of their sites. This is not very common, but if your weblog happens to be the one that finally breaks through into mass public consciousness, you could find yourself shaking hands with strangers at the mall.

Online Privacy in General

I have spent some time detailing the ramifications of an active life online. It is worth pointing out that a surprising amount of information can be easily acquired about almost any individual—whether or not they have an online presence—through a simple Web search. Keeping your name and home address out of online white pages requires quite a concerted effort, and this is true for webloggers and non-webloggers alike. I encourage everyone with computer access to spend an evening or afternoon purging their information from as many online white page directories as they can find.

It's not that the information is new to the Web; it's that the Web makes it readily accessible from any computer around the world. It gives me the creeps to find my name and address on a page with a map to my house and a list of nearby restaurants. If you maintain an active online presence, you may want to take extra care in managing this information; if you have family members who do not spend much time online, take the time to show them how to delete their own information from these online directories.

Fighting Spam

If you publish your email address anywhere on the Web, you will begin to receive spam (unsolicited email advertising a service or product). Whatever the number of spam emails you currently receive, once your page is linked by another site, that number will increase. Spambots (automated computer programs) roam the Web, following every link on every page, logging any email address they find into a database that will be used by clueless marketing departments to send you offers for Viagra, Web design services, and toner for your printer. Then they sell these lists to equally clueless but technically inept individuals who want to send you information on adding inches to or subtracting inches from the body part of your choice—or worse.

There is only one sure way to prevent this: Remove your email address from your site altogether. Some webloggers have replaced the email address with a contact page that contains a form for their readers to use to submit their comments. This arrangement foils the spambots but it may cut down on the amount of reader feedback you receive.

Before you take any drastic step, there are a number of reasonable compromises to consider. Web designers have invented numerous ways of protecting themselves from the wretched spambot while still allowing their readers to reach them. Like any war, this one escalates. With the introduction of any innovative email obfuscation technique, the serious email harvesters contrive a countermeasure. But you can prevent less sophisticated spambots from collecting your email address in various ways. Here are two simple ones:

- Write it out: Designate your email address as yourname at example dot com and let your readers type it out themselves.
- Add a spamblock: Instead of yourname@example.com, use yourname@REMOVESPAMBLOCKexample.com.

I have two email addresses, one for the public and one for family and very close friends. Since the email address you list on your website will never be completely safe from spambots, use it for all of your public correspondence, Usenet postings, mailing lists, and any other activity that may result in your email address being posted to the Web. You won't receive less spam, but you can hope that your private address will remain relatively spam-free.

Check to see how much an additional email address would cost you from your present ISP, or just create a new one using one of the many free services available on the Web. (Note that many of these free services are suspected of selling their customers' information, since these accounts are notorious for receiving spam even when they are listed nowhere and rarely used.)

When, in spite of your best precautions, you receive spam, remember that you have only two good choices: to report it to the offending party's ISP or to a central clearinghouse such as SpamCop, or to discard it. Replying to any spam, especially one that promises to remove you from their mailing list, will only confirm to the sender that they have found a working address, and you will find your inbox filling up with more garbage than ever.

Taking a Break

When you created your site, you anticipated an update schedule based on your circumstances at the time. But your work duties may expand or family responsibilities may necessitate a complete rearrangement of your spare time. Whatever the case, feel free to revise your schedule to meet your needs. If you are maintaining a professional site, you will have to arrange sufficient work hours to enable you to post on a regular basis. If life events dictate that you update your personal site three days a week instead of five, do it. If you can only manage to find a block of three uninterrupted hours once a week, that will have to do. If the situation warrants it, take off a week or three; be ruthless in aligning your priorities to meet the needs of the situation.

You need not go into elaborate detail if you decide to change your schedule or take a break. A simple announcement that you will be updating three times a week or that you will be back in a month is all you need to say. Your audience knows that you produce your site in your spare time, and they understand that your site, while a priority, is not as important as your job or the people you love. In any case, arrange your weblog schedule to suit your life, not the other way around.

What if you have plenty of time to update your weblog, but updating your weblog still feels like a chore? What if you feel harassed by even a reduced schedule? If you begin to feel that you have allowed your weblog to take over your life, it's time to take a break. Place a small announcement on your site stating that you will be taking the next week or two off. There is no need to provide a detailed explanation. Whatever you do, don't go on and on about feeling pressured by your audience to post constantly to your site; it is this very lack of perspective that has turned your pleasant pastime into drudgery.

Now, walk away from the computer.

If, in a day or two, you find yourself wanting to post an entry, that's a good sign. It means that all you needed was a break and it's time to reevaluate your schedule. But wait out the entire week before beginning to post—you really did need a vacation from your site.

Or you may not miss your weblog at all. If you feel relieved to be taking a break, spend some time thinking about what you are relieved from. Were you suffering from information overload? Did you feel a great deal of pressure to read a certain number of sites every day? Have you been posting links to articles that you find only mildly interesting? Were you having trouble thinking of stories to tell?

It may be that all you need is to revise the purpose of your site. Go back again to the idea of an audience of one and try to figure out what you want your site to be. If you find that other subjects or other types of weblogs interest you more than your own, recreate your site to reflect your new vision. Would you like your weblog to be a place to showcase your photography? Do it. Would you like to post extended reflections on one linked article a day? Start writing. Would you like to focus on humorous news stories instead of current events? Have a blast.

Spend your week off thinking about everything you'd like to be doing with your site and then come back and do it. It may be that a simple change like a new design or a new approach to your usual material will rekindle your interest in posting. It may be that you are simply spending too much time on your weblog, and that a reduced schedule will restore balance to your life. You may need to completely revamp your approach and your site. Do whatever it is that will keep your weblog fun and interesting for you.

Or something else may happen. You may not miss it at all. If, during a two-week hiatus, you don't miss maintaining your weblog, do an experiment. Set a day to begin updating again. If that day rolls around and the update is enjoyable, just go on as usual. All you needed was a break.

But if you find yourself dreading the day you sit down again to write your page, it's time to take stock. Your weblog has become tiresome for you. The time investment may be greater than you had anticipated, or you may have discovered a new interest that you would like to pursue instead. If this is the case, just put the weblog aside. Announce that you will no longer be updating your site and then go outside and take a walk.

You may continue using your site as a personal portal, and you may even be moved to post an entry now and then. Once you are completely relieved of the responsibility of regular posting, you might discover that you enjoy maintaining your site on a less ambitious scale. But if it stops being fun, just stop altogether. Your readers will miss you, but life will go on. It is, after all, only a weblog.

I've watched a number of weblogs disappear when their maintainers moved on to other, presumably more rewarding pastimes. I know of others that have been there from the start of the movement and are still going strong. Some of these sites hold to more relaxed schedules than they did back in the day; others are as vigorous as ever. I don't know if the ex-weblog-gers miss their weblogs. I don't know if they ever wish they still had their little spot on the Web, a place to share stories, tell a few jokes, learn a little HTML. I think that I would miss those things, but I wonder if that might someday change.

I know that I will never regret the time I've spent creating and maintaining my site. My weblog has provided me with a reason to write every day, something I never could manage before. In my weblog I have a tool that encourages me to critically evaluate the opinions of others and to carefully articulate my own. Because the format encourages brevity, I am a better writer; because of those space constraints, I have been inspired to move from my weblog to longer forms.

My weblog has provided me with a place to express my views to an audience that is larger than I have ever fit around a table at my local coffeehouse or pub. The fact that they visit my site regularly is gratifying enough; that they have proved to be so thoughtful is beyond expectation. Through my weblog I have made online friends and watched them translate into offline companions. Creating my weblog I have challenged myself. Reading others, I have been informed, infuriated, entertained, and inspired. I am one of a vital community of interesting—and incessantly interested—people. I invite you to join us.

Referenced Websites

Internet Archive	http://www.archive.org/
Spamcop	http://www.spamcop.net/

Spamproofing Your Site

Google resources:	http://directory.google.com/Top/ Computers/Internet/Abuse/ Spam/Preventing/
Hivelogic Email Address Encoder & Javascript Wrapper	http://www.hivelogic.com/ safeaddress/
Thwarting Spambots	http://www.sbw.org/spambot/

Afterword: Another Look Back and a Look Forward

At the beginning of 2000, just a year after coming together, the weblog community was in turmoil. Nothing was going as planned.

In early 1999 the excitement and quick growth of the nascent weblog community had been met almost immediately with a sharp wave of backlash from other online writers. In a piece called "Fear of Links," *Salon* columnist Scott Rosenberg defended the new form against the derision of his fellow journalists, insinuating that their "defensive hostility" stemmed from their need to distinguish their own practice of searching the Web for story leads from the weblog's simple formula of links and commentary.

A few members of the online zine community were openly hostile, accusing weblogs of "navel gazing" and describing them as stupid lists of links. Webloggers, excited by the new form and eager to take their place in the larger online community, were caught off guard. Angry weblog entries pointed the entire community to pieces written by various members of the "personal website mafia," articles that ranged from the antagonistic to the merely snotty. At Slashdot, Jon Katz noted the weblog phenomenon in an article about online communities; the Slashdot community seemed underwhelmed.

Now, this is important, because a discussion of the history of weblogs is more about a community than a form. Slashdot, established in 1997, is often cited as an early weblog, but it is just as often characterized as a discussion forum. Describing their site as "News for Nerds," each day Slashdot's editors post links to interesting articles, newest links at the top. Inside the site community members post their comments. To the unbiased eye, Slashdot is a collaborative weblog with a discussion board, but its place on the Web was well established before the weblog movement took hold, and the two communities never merged.

Those first webloggers soon discovered a community of parallel sites that called themselves E/N pages (for "everything/ nothing," a description of their subject matter). Though they used the same format (dated entries, newest at the top), their focus and sensibility was completely divergent from that of the emerging weblog community. Members of both communities agreed that though the format was identical, the sites, somehow, were different. The E/N and weblog communities remained distinct.

In those first few months of 1999, the weblog community did what all new communities do: sought to consolidate. New weblogs were welcomed enthusiastically into the fold. For a long time, many weblogs posted an entry pointing to any new weblog they found. Mailing lists and community groups were formed. Members debated weblog etiquette, responded to the backlash, and above all sought to answer the question, What is a weblog? Individuals experimented with mixing linkless posts among their normal entries.

Camworld's sidebar, still the definitive list of weblogs, kept growing. After a frustrating attempt to organize the list by type (and responses by webloggers who didn't want to be "boxed in" to categories), Cameron quit the business of cataloguing weblogs and trimmed his list to include only the sites he actually read. In an effort to collect a list in one place, Brigitte Eaton created the Eatonweb portal and solicited URLs. Her reluctance to judge the appropriateness of anyone's effort led to her only criterion: that each site include dated entries. Weblogs, journals, and E/N pages were listed side by side.

The question of definitions became more acute with the introduction of Blogger in August 1999. Though only one of several services that automated weblog updates, Blogger was by far the most visible. The software, simple to use, became widely known as a tool that enabled anyone to publish a weblog, attracting large numbers of users who didn't know HTML. Because it provided no easy interface for adding a link to a post, these new sites contained entry after entry of blurts and personal observations, with few, if any, links to other sites. Because the software used to create the sites was called Blogger, all of those who used it considered their sites to be weblogs.

Weblogs, once about links, were suddenly overshadowed by a large and growing community that was using Blogger to create a completely different kind of site. Literally thousands of new Blogger sites were created in a matter of months. The press swarmed around the company's young, charismatic founders and conflated the publishing tool with the community. Meg Hourihan and Evan Williams, seeking funding for their start-up and happy for any exposure, explained their product and touted their growing user base. Article after article appeared, defining a weblog as a website that was created with Blogger. If Meg or Ev ever said anything to dispel this notion, it never appeared in the published articles.

The weblog community, which had seemed poised for greater visibility, was caught in its own struggle to simultaneously define and extend itself, preserve its identity against the influx of short-form diarists, and defend the form's value to its detractors.

By March 2000, half a dozen new weblog management products, most of them free, had been released. Each of them was reviewed in turn by the weblog community and each was adopted by a contingent of loyal users. Some later products offered greater functionality than Blogger, but few could surpass Blogger's ease of use. UserLand, creator of the software that a few of the old-school webloggers had modified to create their original sites, released Manila, a product that included weblog maintenance features. The press remained focused on Blogger.

Those in the original weblog community who had not converted their sites to the new software were increasingly frustrated. Much of the media coverage identified the Blogger directory, a listing of recently updated Blogger sites, as the portal by which interested readers could find a weblog they liked; many of the old-school and first-wave webloggers, who had helped define the form, felt invisible. Filter-style webloggers watched in dismay as the number of short-form diaries swelled, most of them unaware of the diverse community that had preceded them. The community, fueled by a mania for automatically updated sites and the popularity of the blog, grew too quickly for anyone to track. Weblogs, which in July 1999 had numbered in the dozens, were in the thousands only six months later.

In 2000, the British newspaper *The Guardian* introduced its own weblog, notable as the first effective attempt by traditional media to utilize the form. Editor Chris Alden produced an outstanding site, bringing his readers varied, interesting, insightful stories, presented with a bit of attitude, from all around the Web. It was, for many of us, the weblog we would have created if only we had the time. Alden did something else: He read and credited nonprofessional weblogs. His innate understanding of the weblog as both a form and a democratic community won him numerous supporters in the weblog universe. His editors, sadly, do not seem to have shared his farsightedness; the *Guardian* Weblog today is a sparse collection of topical links.

Webloggers who maintained filters still spoke excitedly about producing guides to the unknown Web and serving as digests for important news. But their message, which had seemed for a year to be on the cusp of wider recognition, was suddenly inaudible, and their creators lacked the means to gain the attention of the press. The original webloggers had spent 1999 perfecting the craft of enticing their readers to click a link; in 2000, many of them felt overshadowed by a sudden accumulation of marginally talented newbies who spent their days posting blurt after mind-numbing blurt. The "weblog mafia" glowered and pronounced that real weblogs were based on links to outside sources, but the bandwagon only gathered speed.

The Eatonweb portal, still growing at a phenomenal rate, may have done much to prevent the community from splintering more than it did. Her decision to allow individuals to identify their sites as weblogs, rather than excluding those who did not meet her criteria, prevented the community from resolving into opposing camps built around link-driven filters and short-form diaries. Eventually, ground down by media confusion and the sheer number of the new sites, even the grouchiest filter webloggers accepted the short-form diary as a species of weblog. But nothing could compensate for the size to which the community had grown.

As 2000 progressed, the explosive growth continued; the sheer size of the community made it impossible even to recognize every weblog by name. What was once a friendly neighborhood had grown to the size of a city; new webloggers established residence and assigned themselves a neighborhood with their links to other weblogs. Subcommunities, or weblog clusters, formed around weblog management tools, shared professions, shared interests and political views, and even geography. In an effort to navigate the growing weblog universe, webrings were formed. "Webloggers," "women webloggers,"

"GLBT webloggers," and others sought to reinforce identities and social alliances within the larger group.

For some people, the size of the community created an interest in tracking the spread of memes (virulently popular ideas) and social relationships among the webloggers themselves. Early backlash against weblogs often accused them of "linking to each other" and "linking to the same things." Turning this criticism on its head, Michael Stillwell created the Beebo Metalog, which tracked the URLs most frequently linked by the weblogs, and the Beebo Weblog Ratings, which measured which weblogs were linked by the most other webloggers. Meanwhile, Jim Aspnes's Weblog Scoop Index tracked which weblogs beat the others to popular links, or as one weblogger put it, who was creating memes, and who was spreading them. The Weblog Scoop Index also listed the top one hundred most popular links of the last twenty-four hours.

Weblog update trackers were created to replace the Eatonweb portal, now grown to unmanageable size. Websites rated individual weblogs' update frequency and designated those who updated most often "power bloggers." For many people, the focus of the weblog went from strength of content to frequency of updates; the idea of the weblog as a publication that came out once a day had disappeared almost entirely.

By the end of 2000, the fragmented community no longer agreed on anything but the shared format of their sites.

◇ ◇ ◇

In 1999 there was nothing new about the weblog. What was new that year was the community that formed around this kind of site. When the Web was new, such lists of links were necessary to point interested readers to the relatively few things that were available. That anything existed on the Web was exciting. Those original lists were based on the idea of scarcity; without pointers, the reader couldn't hope to find the new things that were available.

The Web in 1999 was a changed place. Overcome with commercial interests and burgeoning with independent creative efforts, the Web had become so large that no portal or search engine could even hope to catalogue it entirely. What the earliest webloggers shared was a fascination with the new medium, an insatiable desire to scour the shelves of this enormous virtual library, and a relentless drive to share with anyone who was interested the things they had found. That they independently structured their pages in the same way is a coincidence of convenience: The behavior of Web browsers demands that for easy access, new material be put on top.

The group of people who came together in 1999 quickly (and, I think, unconsciously) recognized the advantages of being part of an online community, and immediately began to use their new network to their collective advantage. They credited one another. They carried on public conversations from site to site. They drew readers by sending them to reliably interesting material all across the Web, and then pointed them to other "sites like mine," thus merging their audiences and expanding their influence.

United by their belief in the value of information exchange, old-school and first-wave filter webloggers eagerly embraced their new community. Their conscious participation in this newly formed group led some to accuse the webloggers of being interested primarily in themselves, but from my perspective, it was really more a matter of enthusiasm. It really seemed as though the sky was the limit, and that joined together, we could somehow change the world. It is ironic that the filter webloggers later criticized the new wave of blogs in identical terms. Their high visibility and enormous numbers caused resentment among more experienced webloggers who felt the new blogs had co-opted their movement. The resentment is understandable. Though they identified themselves as "weblogs," the blogs focused their attention on the social aspects of the community, inverting the primary values of the original community.

The backlash against the original weblog community was perhaps inevitable. Writers who had transferred their work into Web sites were still thinking in terms of an old-media broadcast model. That the Web has the ability to reach millions of people is its amazing potential. No other medium extends so far. To imagine that one man or woman, with minor expense, could gain the attention of an unlimited audience was seductive. But in fact, audiences in the new medium are more limited. On paper, a writer is guaranteed a circulation, a determined number of copies to be printed and distributed. In television and radio, programs vie for time in a finite schedule, but the number of competing broadcasts is comparatively low. The old media system has channels of distribution that place content before the available audience. Whether or not an individual column is read or a show is watched is a function of scarcity; media consumers select from among a limited number of choices.

The Web has no such scarcity and no such distribution channels. Because each website is just one in a sea of millions, individuals who publish on the Web will always be limited in their ability to get their work in front of an audience. The dot-coms taught us that brand recognition was most effectively gained through advertising and publicity in established, old-media outlets.

When both the zinesters and early filter webloggers read articles that drew attention to sites that appeared to require only a modicum of effort, it must have been frustrating, especially to anyone who had not yet come to terms with the realities of independent online publishing. On the Web, an independent publisher cannot be assured of having a large audience, ever. The payoff is that those who do come do so deliberately. These micro-audiences grow slowly, but they are devoted. This error in thinking is forgivable: It takes time and experience to understand the properties of any new medium.

For some reason, the charges made against weblogs by early critics crop up again and again, consistently enough that it is no longer possible to dismiss them strictly as sour grapes. From a distance weblogs can appear to be effortless endeavors, created by people convinced that social connections are the equivalent of content. Such criticism does not acknowledge the way in which weblogs reflect the fundamental attributes of the Web itself.

What critics dismiss as easy linking, webloggers understand as information foraging, filtering, and contextualization. When critics complain that weblogs aren't real writing, webloggers point out that concision is difficult, and rare. Detractors complain about incestuous linking; webloggers emphasize the ability of grassroots networks to organize and amplify individual voices on the Web. Those who grumble at seeing the same site linked on a dozen weblogs rail against the most fundamental attribute of the Web itself—its ability to allow people to share information easily. And those who decry cross-blog talk have not yet understood the value of bringing a dozen lively minds to bear upon the same subject.

◇ ◇ ◇

So what happened next?

At the beginning of 2001, Pyra, the company that created Blogger, imploded. Citing irreconcilable differences, the company broke up, leaving only one of its founders to manage the community that, together, they had grown. The high-tech bubble burst. Masses of people, webloggers among them, were thrown onto the job market, hired by new companies, and then thrown out of work again as the reality of the postbubble economy set in. Many webloggers migrated to newer weblog management systems, uncertain of Blogger's future or seduced by larger feature sets. Others stubbornly stuck with what they were using, praying that their favorite service would live to see another day; in the new "New Economy," free was no longer a business plan, and nothing was certain to last. And still more new weblogs appeared.

It's hard to tell if the growth of the weblog community leveled off a bit in 2001, or if the community just became so large that from the inside it was no longer possible to perceive the expansion. Comment systems were widely adopted throughout the community, allowing individual weblogs to cultivate the small communities that had collected around their sites. Two new weblog tracking services were introduced in 2001. Daypop, a search engine for "the living Web," was specifically designed to catalogue weblogs and news services to create a real-time search engine. Cameron Marlow of MIT's Media Lab began work on Blogdex, which seeks to track the spread of memes through the weblog community and to map the complex social relationships that shape the weblog universe.

The aftermath of September 11 illustrated the power of unmediated storytelling, as survivors shared eyewitness accounts of the great tragedy on their weblogs. Filter weblogs once again rose to the forefront, drawing larger audiences than ever before and illustrating definitively the power and utility of the human filter. September 11 also spawned a generation of "warblogs," mostly hawkish sites that focused on the U.S. response to the terrorist attacks. The warblogs also brought a contingent of conservative and libertarian voices into the historically left-leaning community.

Post-September 11 brought us another well-done weblog from the mainstream media, the *Christian Science Monitor*'s A Changed World. Updated daily, A Changed World synopsized the news of current U.S. antiterrorist efforts, mixing links to their own content with links to material from other online news outlets. It is a rare example of a mainstream media publication using the weblog format as successfully as its amateur progenitors.

The year 2001 saw an increasing number of filters being used by their maintainers as personal op-ed pages. The op-ed filter provides links for reference, but it exists primarily as a platform for the maintainer to proclaim her views.

A few minor celebrities discovered the power of the weblog to connect with and consolidate their fan base. Actor Wil Wheaton and entertainer RuPaul created classic blogs, discussing their lives and philosophies, and author Neil Gaiman used his to update his fans on his progress in writing and, later, promoting his latest book.

A few professional columnists began maintaining weblogs in 2001. As might be expected, most of these are op-ed filters, enabling their maintainers to respond to news events more rapidly than their regular columns would allow. Predictably, this trend set off another flurry of speculation about weblogs as journalism. While the weblog is an ideal format for this type of instant response, those who point to the "pro-bloggers" as harbingers of a new form of journalism have forgotten that these columnists gained whatever influence they might have under the auspices of traditional old-media. In that world, influence—or the chance to earn it—is bestowed from above. Writers are hired, featured, and promoted by large media outlets that leverage their own brand-recognition and distribution to create audiences for their writers. That the pro-bloggers attract readers may testify to their talent, but it is a demonstration of celebrity, not the power of the new form.

There is nothing revolutionary about writing short daily pieces, and pundits have seemingly always been more concerned with the views of their colleagues than with the pulse of the people. Too many pro-bloggers approach the form from a distinctly old-media point of view, rarely linking to any of the intelligent, informed individuals in the larger weblog community. Instead, they link to each other, as if only other journalists have anything worthwhile to say. Without question, the weblog format can be used effectively in traditional journalism, but the weblog movement is about the ability of everyday people to say their own piece. The revolution, when it comes, will be different from this.

Too many pro-bloggers have not understood the weblog in another way: They link only to those pieces with which they agree, often declining to link to the articles and speeches they denounce.

Weblogs can be used to promote particular points of view, certainly, but the weblog method—which demands a link to any referenced material that can be found online—ensures a level of accountability not found in traditional media. Snippets of commentary that do not link to their primary sources are not a form of "new journalism"—they are merely more frequent instances of an intellectually bankrupt form of old journalism (though, of course, this is not really responsible journalism at all).

These sites have adopted the weblog format but lack the understanding—or courage—to apply the method. These "weblogs" represent neither journalism nor weblogs; they are simple vehicles for self-promotion. Weblogs have historically—in the hands of amateurs—had more courage and intellectual integrity than this.

In early 2002 one of the pro-bloggers wrote that, to the best of her knowledge, in 2001 she had invented what was now known as the weblog. Receiving a quick reaction from the wider weblog community, she was surprised to discover that she had not, and that webloggers covered the entire political spectrum and came from all walks of life. The incident was regarded as an example of the arrogance of well-heeled old-media newcomers coopting the new, democratic genre for their own self-promotion, but a similar statement could just as easily have come from the center of any of the newer weblog clusters, so balkanized is the community today.

◇ ◇ ◇

As I write these words, the weblog movement is three years old. The community has grown beyond our wildest expectations and the form itself has been redefined in ways we never anticipated.

I love the ways in which people have expanded the form. I love seeing people apply the weblog concept in ways I don't expect. I love the project weblogs, the photo weblogs, the historical weblogs, and the weblog that was created so that two guys could discuss Wittgenstein. It has given me great pleasure to watch more than one terrible weblog transform into one of the best, just by virtue of its maintainer writing every day. I love watching webloggers gain the confidence and the discipline to start new projects. I love watching weblogs change and grow.

The blog and notebook are strong. New ones are created every day, and as a whole, these subgenres have been quietly absorbed into the larger community. I would like to see a little more mixing between the blogs and the filters; it seems sometimes that the two styles of weblog coexist in separate but equal universes. The focus on the weblog as a vehicle of personal expression has been both good and bad for the community. This focus has encouraged people to freely express their opinions on everything from film to politics to their morning cup of coffee. This is a change from the early days when some filter editors had to be encouraged to give us a little more information about the links they were posting.

On the other hand there are now few examples of the pithiness and concision that used to inform the weblog community. The best weblogs have always exhibited a strong point of view, whether or not their maintainers have chosen to explicitly voice their opinions. More words are not always more clear, and not every link needs to be explained at length. While I value the opinions of my fellow webloggers, I would remind them that the inclusion of a link often says much by itself, and that personality is more sharply revealed by actions than through words.

I see fewer and fewer curiosity cabinets. Most of the new webloggers, it seems, are interested in direct self-expression of one kind or another, and few are simply driven to "find the good stuff" and share. I miss the playfulness that was once so common, and the sense of adventure that prevailed among the creators of this kind of site.

Connections between the English-speaking community of webloggers and those in different countries are still rare. In addition to the weblog communities in the United States, Canada, the United Kingdom, Australia, and the Netherlands, I have seen weblogs in French, Italian, German, Russian, Spanish, Greek, Icelandic, Hebrew, and Swedish. For most Americans, a language barrier restricts our communications with webloggers from other countries, but individuals on all sides can help to bridge that gap.

Op-ed blogs have coalesced as an important subgenre since the September 11 attacks. But like the political commentators they emulate, too many of them focus on proving that their opponents are wrong or stupid instead of seeking the truth. When television's *McLaughlin Group* and others like it first appeared, this approach was entertaining, I suppose, in an appalling, train-wreck sort of way. On all of these shows, closed minds and heavy-handed insults masquerade as vigorous discussion.

I have found it disheartening to see this style of discourse creep onto the editorial pages of our newspapers and into the mouths of politicians themselves, only to be amplified by an undiscerning press. Defending one's "side" at all costs does no service to the people—and ideals—that really matter. Who benefits from such

tactics? Only the very wealthy and very powerful. Not government. Not the People. Even the columnists and commentators
who employ these tactics do not gain enough to offset the
tremendous damage they do to the political process itself.

I suppose it is natural that some webloggers would adopt this
style after seeing it presented for so many years as a legitimate
model of political discourse. Is it fair to expect motivated amateurs to discern the insubstantiality of this mode of rhetoric
when professional news editors seemingly cannot? But I can't
help being unhappy to see so many fine minds wasted on the intellectual equivalent of the World Wrestling Federation. There
are still intellectually honest journalists and political commentators working in the mainstream media; let them be the model
for our approach.

I would love to see a new wave of op-ed bloggers who build
their cases on reason rather than rhetorical attacks. Let the next
wave evaluate information according to its truth, not its political expediency. Let them strive for clarity and refute obfuscation from all sides. Passion need not be unreasonable, and
strong opinion need not be obstinate. Let the next generation
of op-ed weblogs show the way.

Filters are stronger than ever. There are impressive foragers
working today, tracking down link after link on news, current
events, popular culture, and art. Professional and subject-specific filters continue to appear, but many more subjects would
still benefit from having a definitive resource. General-interest
filters are as popular as ever; I am amazed at the quality and variety among the new ones I find. Where the first wave of general-interest filters included frequent links to technology-related
news, three years later the subject matter has become broader,
with most of these sites linking generously to general-interest
news articles and analysis instead.

But even these sites have been infected with the rhetorical
posturing of the day. In too many cases, shrill self-righteousness

has replaced the snarkiness that infused the first-wave weblogs. Snarkiness isn't the best approach to changing the world, I guess. But neither is full-blown sarcasm or self-congratulatory bombast. I firmly believe that webloggers have a serious contribution to make to political and cultural discourse by filtering and contextualizing information, but pounding relentlessly on the same drum will change no one's mind.

I see a danger in the direction that many of these filters have chosen. In *Data Smog*, author David Shenk names as his Eighth Law: "Birds of a feather flock virtually together," articulating the situation I see facing many of the weblog clusters that have formed in the past year: "There is a great danger here of mistaking cultural tribalism for real, shared understanding. . . . A pluralistic democracy requires a certain amount of tolerance and consensus, rooted in the ability to understand a wide variety of perspectives and agree on common questions."

Webloggers interested in political matters—on both the left and the right—seem more and more to exist in echo chambers of their own making, linking and reading only weblogs and other publications that reflect back their own points of view. The weblog possesses an unmatched ability to create targeted serendipity by presenting its self-selected audience with news and trivia that is predictably interesting and useful. But the very idea of serendipity demands that the discoveries so provided be to some extent unexpected. When news stories are rigorously selected to align with a predetermined worldview, human filters become little more than propaganda machines.

Automated news aggregators are inferior to human filters because they unavoidably leave vast expanses of the world unconsidered—but then again, they do not pretend to represent the world. A man who has a computer filter to him only information about golf and cigars may forget about the NBA playoffs, but he will not imagine that his view of the world is complete.

By clustering too closely together, webloggers risk amplifying their own view of the world to an extent that distorts their perception of reality. To my mind, these constructed bubbles have the potential to be far more dangerous than any mindless electronic feed. It is natural to congregate with others who share our point of view. This is the basis of community (even geographical communities, which literally view the world from a shared physical space). There is obvious value in conversing with others of like mind. Supportive communities reinforce and strengthen common values and provide a base of action for individual members. The danger arises when ideological weblogs cluster so tightly that they entertain no other views. By self-referentially reflecting numerous versions of a comfortable or sanctioned description of the facts, such systems appear to present a nuanced representation of the world, while actually oversimplifying its complexity.

In the twenty-first century the world demands that we broaden our view, not narrow it further. We have in the weblog an unprecedented tool with which to share ideas and understand other worldviews, but this opportunity is squandered when we deliberately shield ourselves from differing points of view. I would like to see more weblogs that use their unique capabilities to illuminate the news, not just promote a familiar point of view. I would like to see a wave of truth seekers who ask hard questions and sort through available perspectives in an attempt to synthesize a truer, more accurate version of the facts than we can rely on from any one source. I would like to see more webloggers seek out opposing viewpoints in order to genuinely consider the different ways in which thoughtful people regard the world.

A weblog is a bully pulpit, and the insightful weblogger has an opportunity to elucidate and navigate the unknown for his readers instead of pulling the gate shut behind them. The webloggers have always been Web travelers. Let us bring home thoughtful stories of little-understood cultures, especially when that culture belongs to the man next door.

Notably, weblogs that focus on a shared profession rarely exhibit this closed-mindedness or lack of respect with regard to dissenting opinion. They eagerly link to one another, disagree vigorously and respectfully, and are willing to test their ideas against the differing ideas of their colleagues. Sometimes they simply state their opposing opinions and leave it to the reader to decide. In the world of professional weblogs, disagreement is a virtue, but disrespect and animosity are not tolerated. This was one of the oldest and finest characteristics of the old-school weblogs, and the current community loses if they let it fall away.

If you asked me what the weblog community needs, I would answer, Stronger ties among webloggers from various clusters, more independent thinkers, and more irreverence. Much, much more irreverence. Everyone seems to take themselves so seriously. I would look for more seekers of truth to offset the proclaimers of right and wrong from all sides of the political spectrum. More open minds. More listeners. A renewed sense of fun. We can never go back to the days when we all knew each other, but I think we can reasonably aspire to become closer than we are. We share so much. Let us use our weblogs to define ourselves individually as we move forward together as a community, joined by our shared commitment to self-expression, free speech, and the vigorous exchange of ideas.

Referenced Books

Shenk, David. *Data Smog: Surviving the Information Glut*, rev. and upd. (New York: HarperCollins, HarperEdge, 1998), 123, 127.

Referenced Websites

Fear of Links, Scott Rosenberg	http://www.salon.com/tech/col/rose/1999/05/28/weblogs/
Here Come the Weblogs, Jon Katz	http://slashdot.org/features/99/05/13/1832251.shtml
Manila	http://manila.userland.com/
Guardian weblog	http://www.guardian.co.uk/weblog/
Beebo Metalog (Internet Archive)	http://web.archive.org/web/20000816034854/beebo.org/metalog/
Beebo Weblog Ratings (Internet Archive)	http://web.archive.org/web/20000815223308/beebo.org/metalog/ratings/
Weblog Scoop Index (Internet Archive)	http://web.archive.org/web/20000520094558/ http://pine.cs.yale.edu/blogs/scoops.html
Daypop	http://www.daypop.com/
Blogdex	http://blogdex.media.mit.edu/
A Changed World	http://www.csmonitor.com/specials/sept11/dailyUpdate.html
WIL WHEATON DOT NET	http://www.wilwheaton.net/
Rupaul's weblog	http://www.rupaul.com/weblog.shtml
Neil Gaiman's journal	http://www.neilgaiman.com/journal/journal.asp

Appendix I:
Creating a Practice Weblog

The best way to start a weblog is to jump right in and get your feet wet. Below are step-by-step directions for creating a practice weblog using Blog*Spot, a free Web hosting service that uses the Blogger weblog tool.

I chose Blog*Spot because the service is free and doesn't require that you download any software. If you are new to weblogging, becoming familiar with Blogger will better enable you to evaluate the functionality and features of the many other tools that are available. More importantly, you will be able to create for yourself a place to learn about weblogging.

Dozens of weblog tools are now available. Once you've had a chance to play around with your practice weblog, I encourage you to investigate the many other possibilities. You may find that Blogger is perfect for you, or you may find that a different tool is better suited to your needs or your way of working. Many webloggers have moved through several tools as their needs have changed and their technical expertise has increased. Have fun!

1. Go to http://www.blogger.com.

2. In the right-hand column, find the box that says "Sign Up." Type in a username and a password. (You will need to type the password twice for verification.)

3. The next screen will ask for:

First Name
Last Name
Organization (you may leave this blank if you like)
Email Address

While you are on this page, take a minute to read the terms of service and then submit your information.

4. You will be sent back to the top page. In the right-hand column, look for a box that says "Your Blogs." Click "Create a New Blog."

5. The next screen will ask you for the title of your new weblog and a description. It will also ask you whether your weblog should be public. For now, choose no. You can change all of this information later.

6. The next screen will ask you whether you would like to host your weblog on your own Web host, or host it on Blog*Spot. Choose Blog*Spot.

7. The next screen will ask you to choose the URL for your weblog. Type in the name of your weblog, or your own name if you prefer (or some other catchy word). Read the terms of service (a new window will open) and check the box to agree.

8. Choose a template.

9. You're signed up! Now, type something in the upper text box. Post this entry by clicking "post and publish," found on the upper right above the text box. Your entry will appear in the bottom half of the screen. Click "view webpage" to see how it looks (a new window will open).

10. Now, start having fun!

Find listings of weblog tools at:

Weblog Madness—Roll Your Own
http://www.larkfarm.com/wlm/roll_your_own.htm

Appendix II:
Adding Links to Your Weblog

The links that connect one webpage to another are called hypertext. Hypertext links together the World Wide Web. It is not necessary that your weblog be link-driven in order to be good, but when you are writing on the World Wide Web, you should know how to make a link and how to frame it effectively.

Capturing a URL

In order to create a link to another site, you will need to include the URL. The easiest way to capture a URL is as follows:

1. Place your cursor in the address window of your browser. This should highlight the entire URL.

2. If it does not, click the button on your mouse or place your cursor at the beginning of the URL (right before it says "http") and drag it to the end of the URL so that it is highlighted.

3. Going to your browser menu, select Edit → Copy.

4. You have now captured the URL. You may now paste it into any document that supports the cut and paste functions.

Constructing a Link

1. Type <a href="

2. Place your cursor immediately following the " and paste the URL by going to your menu and choosing Edit → Paste. It will look like this: <a href="http://www.yahoo.com

3. Type "> like this:
   <a href="http://www.yahoo.com">

4. Type the words you want to link, like this:
   <a href="http://www.yahoo.com">my favorite site

5. Type </a> so that it looks like this:
   <a href="http://www.yahoo.com">my favorite site</a>

6. When it appears in a Web browser, it will look like this:
   <u>my favorite site</u>
   . . . and when you click on it, it will take you to Yahoo!.

7. Now, look at the link in your Web browser. Remember to click the link to make sure it works. If you leave out even one quotation mark or bracket, the link will not work. Check also to see that it goes where you intended it to go. On more than one occasion I have accidentally pasted the wrong URL into a link, rendering my linktext meaningless!

Writing Linktext

Writing in hypertext is different in some ways from writing on the page. It's more efficient, for one thing. In text, if I wished to cite another book, I would have to say: "In Chapter One of his book *The Wealth of Nations* Adam Smith states . . ." and then quote as much of his book as I needed and as copyright law would allow. On the Web, I have many more choices. If *The Wealth of Nations* existed online, I would be able to point my readers to the entire book and possibly to the specific sections I was most interested in. I could even link to the book as an aside and use my entire text to make a point completely unrelated to the substance of Smith's work.

Webloggers who regularly link to other sites explore daily the ways in which hypertext can be used most effectively. Here are a few examples of common styles of weblog linktext that can serve as springboards in your own exploration of hypertext writing.

If this were the Web, I could create actual links to illustrate the principles I delineate. Because this is a book, we will just pretend. In the examples that follow, underlined text will stand for a link on a webpage, and bold text will be used to refer to that "link."

Visual Considerations

Because hyperlinks are often underlined, I structure sentences to avoid linking commas, periods, and other baseline punctuation. If a sentence ends with a link, I close the link before <u>adding the period</u>. There's no rule that says I need to do that—underlined commas and periods just look funny to me.

I also favor shorter links over longer ones. I think <u>shorter links</u> just look better than long ones, especially when <u>a long link extends across more than one line</u>.

These rules are based purely on what looks best to my eye. Use your own judgment to create links that look good to you.

Literal Hypertext

Sometimes a link says exactly what it is. Writing this kind of linktext doesn't require much imagination, but it makes it easier for a reader to tell where a link will take him. This type of link may be used to direct the reader to another site, to make a reference clear, or as a sort of afterthought.

Senator Toughenough's latest article, <u>Why We Can No Longer Afford to Tolerate the Left</u>, exactly reflects my views on foreign and domestic policy.

Why We Can No Longer Afford to Tolerate the Left links to an article of the same name.

I saw <u>Julie</u> walking past the store the other day.

Julie links to Julie's personal site.

There was a <u>smidgen</u> of caviar left on the bed of carrot flambé.

smidgen links to the word's definition in an online dictionary.

Summarizing Linktext

Summarizing linktext tries to give the reader enough information to decide whether to click through the link. The writer may do this by quoting the article's title, highlighting an interesting or representative section of the article, or creating his own summary of the article.

When a title or headline is very descriptive, weblog editors often use it as their entire linktext.

<u>Why We Can No Longer Afford to Tolerate the Left</u>

Why We Can No Longer Afford to Tolerate the Left links to an article of the same name.

Sometimes the title of the article is not very descriptive; then the weblogger may choose to quote an interesting or representative piece of text, with or without the title.

> "As you read and think and write daily, you will quickly find that you are smarter, more interesting, and more articulate than you <u>ever dreamed you could be</u>."

ever dreamed you could be links to Chapter 4 of this book.

> <u>Finding Your Voice</u>
>
> As you read and think and write daily, you will quickly find that you are smarter, more interesting, and more articulate than you ever dreamed you could be.

Finding Your Voice links to Chapter 4 of this book.

Sometimes webloggers prefer to explain the gist of the article themselves. They may feel that the headline doesn't give enough information or accurately convey the meaning of the article, or they may want to articulate their own interpretation.

> Rebecca Blood reflects on the <u>qualities that make a weblog memorable</u> and concludes that the best weblogs are written to please only their maintainers.

qualities that make a weblog memorable links to Chapter 4 of this book.

You can have the best of both worlds by summarizing, then introducing a pull quote to give the flavor of the writing.

> Rebecca Blood reflects on the <u>qualities that make a weblog memorable</u> and concludes that the best weblogs are written to please only their maintainers.
>
>> If you want to create a compelling weblog, you must write for an audience of one: yourself.
>>
>> The audience of one is the single most important principle behind creating a website—indeed, anything—that is fresh, interesting, and compelling.

qualities that make a weblog memorable links to Chapter 4 of this book.

Conversational Linktext

Because weblog readers come to know their weblog editors, webloggers have a certain amount of latitude in constructing linktext. Once a reader comes to trust—or at least know—a weblogger's preferences, he may be willing to click a link that is not fully descriptive of the site it points to. Nearly everyone hates a link that says "Check this out," but on a weblog, linktext can provide considerably less complete information than on a professional site and still inspire its readers to take a chance.

Webloggers often use their linktext to state an opinion instead of the facts.

> <u>More proof</u> that Sen. Terrance Toughenough is Evil.

More proof points to an article enumerating campaign contributions from a prominent maker of pesticides made to Toughenough just weeks before he introduced legislation that would exempt chemical manufacturers from environmental regulation.

Sometimes just a modicum of information about what the reader can expect is enough.

Mr. Harshalot <u>reviews</u> the Latest Fantasy Epic Film.

reviews points to another scathing review by well-known cantankerous film reviewer Mr. Harshalot.

Once in a while you may rely on your reputation for stellar links and simply give your readers a hint of what they may expect if they click a link. Be warned that if you do this very frequently, people may tire of it unless your linktext itself is very entertaining all on its own.

<u>Funniest. Website. Ever.</u>

Funniest. Website. Ever. points to http://www.brunching.com/. Trust me.

(Yes, I know I broke my own rule about periods in that last link. But if I had constructed the links around each individual word, readers might reasonably expect to visit a different website with each click. Be funny, be flexible, and break your own rules once in a while.)

Appendix III: Nuts and Bolts

Weblog Management Tools

All of the available weblog tools are essentially specialized content management systems. They allow you to make entries, save them to your archives, add permalinks, and upload all of it to your server. Most, if not all of them, also do the HTML for you, so that once your template is set up, all you have to do is write the words, add the link, and click a button to make it appear on your weblog. All of them have been designed to make updating and maintaining your weblog as easy as possible, and most of them are low-cost or free.

Below are descriptions of the basic types of weblog management software, followed by a few examples. These examples are intended merely as illustrations and should not be interpreted as recommendations. There are many more software packages available! The best tool for you may not be mentioned here. See Chapter 3 for guidelines on evaluating and choosing a weblog management tool.

WEB-HOSTED SYSTEMS: These tools do almost everything for you. They provide you with a special webpage where you can post, format, and delete entries on a weblog that is hosted by the service itself. All you need do is sign up, and these services provide you with your own place on the Web. Your weblog may have a banner ad at the top, and your URL will always include the name of your weblog service. When you use these services, you usually get much, much more than you pay for, but occasionally access to your weblog may become slow or sporadic.

Examples: Blog*Spot, Pitas

WEB-BASED SYSTEMS: Like Web-hosted systems, these services provide you with a Web-based interface that allows you to post, format, and edit your weblog entries. The difference is that your site must be hosted elsewhere. Since updating your site is handled through the system's central computer, these services can sometimes be slow.

Example: Blogger

SELF-INSTALLED SYSTEMS: These are software packages that you download and run on your own computer or Web server. This ensures that you will not be subject to slowdowns or outages caused by high traffic to a central server. These packages may require some technical expertise.

Examples: Radio UserLand (runs on your own computer); Greymatter, Movable Type (run on your Web server)

HAND CODING: Some Luddite webloggers resist any form of automation and insist on hand coding their sites by typing HTML into a text editor. Some of them, more amenable to modern ways, may use a Web-authoring tool such as Dreamweaver, but the result is always the same: They connect to their Web hosts and FTP the results to their websites. Someone who updates his site by hand either enjoys coding or none of the available software quite suits his needs. Hand coding provides the weblogger with complete control over the style and arrangement of his entries. Unless the weblogger is technically advanced enough to implement open-source software like PHP or write his own weblog management system, this approach may entail a certain loss of efficiency since archives must be updated and posted manually.

Web Hosts

If you choose not to use one of the weblog services that offer you Web space, or if you find that you have outgrown such services, you will need to secure free space elsewhere or purchase server space from a dedicated Web hosting service.

First, investigate the terms of your current ISP; your account may entitle you to a small amount of Web space for a personal site. Though limited, this space is likely to be perfectly adequate for a text-oriented weblog.

If your account does not allow you to maintain a personal website, free space is available from some of the larger corporate sites like Yahoo!. A Google search for ["free Web hosting"] will produce a list of such services. Like some of the free weblog services, these sites come with an ad at the top—sometimes an annoying pop-up ad, to boot. Only you can decide whether this is an acceptable price to pay for free hosting.

If you get really serious about your weblog, you may want to spend money on dedicated space for your site. This is an option even if you are not ready to purchase your own domain. When you buy dedicated Web hosting without your own domain, your URL will look something like this: yourname.example.com. Once you have your own domain, you will definitely need to arrange for dedicated server space to host your weblog. When choosing a Web host, you need to consider seven major areas:

COST: Shop around. You do not need to pay an excessive amount for server space. Compare various packages until you find one that offers the features you need at the lowest cost. Reasonable offerings are available even for those of us who are not technical gods.

RELIABILITY: Make this your top priority. If the computer your website is hosted on breaks down or loses its connection to the Web, no one will be able to visit your site. If your Web host does not spend your money to pay highly skilled professionals to keep their computer equipment in top-notch condition, you are wasting your money. Why pay for sporadic service?

Furthermore, anyone who lacks the technical expertise to ensure that their servers work reliably (and are quickly repaired when something goes wrong) may also lose your account information or otherwise make your life miserable. Do not patronize any Web host who will not promise close to 100 percent up-time.

SERVER SPACE: Your server space allotment is how much data you are allowed to store on your host's computer. Generally, graphics and photographs are larger than HTML files. MP3s and videos are larger still.

If your current host does not enable you to see how large your files are, you may want to download the files to your home computer to measure for yourself (just note the file sizes and add them up). Unless you plan to post numerous photographs or other graphics-heavy material, you will not need a huge allotment. I would say that 20–30 MB is plenty for a weblog. Give yourself enough space to grow at a reasonable rate for the next year or two.

BANDWIDTH: Bandwidth measures how much data is pulled from your website onto all of the computers that look at your site. If ten people look at your 2 MB file, your bandwidth usage will be 20 MB; if three people look at your 10 MB page of photographs, your bandwidth usage will be 30 MB. It's a combination of the size of your files and the traffic your site receives.

Unless you are wildly popular, bandwidth will probably never be an issue for you. I have never gone over my bandwidth allotment, even on my highest day, when my site was visited by fifteen hundred visitors. If I had maintained that level of traffic for an entire month (or even two weeks), perhaps I would have. If your site is graphics-heavy, your bandwidth usage will be much higher than mine is for a comparable number of page views.

Be aware that most lower-cost Web hosting packages will charge you for every MB of usage above your allotment and that you have no control over the traffic your site will receive. Occasionally a personal site will be linked by a massively influential website or its URL will be passed incessantly through email (remember All Your Base?). For sites with a limited allocation of bandwidth, this sudden surge in popularity can mean significant additional charges, and in a few cases site owners have been forced to remove their sites from the Web, unable to afford their own popularity. A high bandwidth allotment is insurance against this ever happening to you. On the other hand, it's unlikely that your site will become this year's most popular meme. Do your own cost-benefit analysis and weight this factor accordingly.

SERVER LOGS: This is a record of your site traffic. Any reputable Web hosting service should offer you server logs (often referred to as "Web logs," by the way, a term that predates the kind of website you now maintain). I would mistrust any Web host that didn't make your statistics available: I would be afraid that they were technically inept. They clearly would not be interested in attracting professional-level clients who would insist on these statistics in order to track the effectiveness of their websites. (Note that your server logs add up rather more quickly than you would ever expect; if you don't want to use up all your disk space, regularly process your log files and get them off your server.)

ADDITIONAL FEATURES: Some hosting packages offer CGI scripting, telnet, crontab files, and the like. If your weblog management software requires CGI scripting or some other specialized functionality, consider only Web hosting packages that include that capability. Otherwise, if you don't know what it is, you probably don't need it. Pay only for what you will use.

SUPPORT: Does your hosting service offer support forums, FAQs, and good email support for its customers? Poke around the site and read the documentation about their services. It's important that you can easily find help when you need it, and that you can understand the help that is available. If the documentation is too technical, look elsewhere. Some hosting services are not intended for the general consumer, and they may not be very responsive to email questions they consider trivial. Look for clear directions and a promise of quick support via email.

When you are choosing a Web hosting service, evaluate both your current needs and those of the foreseeable future. Read the technical specs of your weblog management software to ensure that you are considering only businesses that can accommodate your needs. If you maintain a private weblog for a finite audience, your current bandwidth allotment will be plenty unless you plan to increase the number of photos, videos, and graphics on your site.

Choose a package that gives you the fewest unnecessary features with the best reliability and support, for the lowest available price. When choosing between cost and reliability, choose reliability. Ask around. Other webloggers are looking for the same things you are: low cost and reliable service. I would judge that the average text-oriented weblog would find 30–50 MB of disk space and 50 MB/day of bandwidth to be perfectly adequate.

For your comparison, Rebecca's Pocket consists of a weblog, three years of archives, and pages and pages of additional links. My site usually updates only once a day and has only one graphic, the header. It currently uses about 20 MB of disk space. In March 2002 I received 800–1,600 unique IPs (with 1,400–3,100 page views) every weekday and 550–950 unique IPs (with 1,154–1,816 page views) on Saturdays and Sundays. My bandwidth usage for the entire month was 1,578 MB, averaging 51 MB a day.

Buying a Domain

After you have maintained your site for several months, your enthusiasm undiminished by the travails of daily updates, you may find that you long for a permanent online home, or you may just want a shorter URL. It might be time to buy some Web space and set up your own domain.

A domain is the name of a site followed by an extension like .com, .net, or .org. So yahoo.com and yahoo.org are different domains since they are followed by different extensions, usually called TLDs (top level domains).

Be aware that managing your own domain, while not rocket science, requires a higher level of technical expertise than does maintaining a weblog hosted by a free service. Many Web hosts and registrars work hard to make it as easy as possible, but the whole business can be very confusing. Look for clear instructions and good documentation in choosing these service providers.

First, choose a Web host. Once you find a domain name, you will want to move quickly, so know who will be hosting your site before you secure the domain. Read their procedures for hosting your domain; your host should provide clear instructions for transferring a domain. Set up an account with your chosen Web host before you purchase the domain.

Your next task will be finding an available domain. Most common words are taken, and so are many uncommon ones. You probably will want either your name or weblog name reflected in your own personal domain. Start by searching the whois database to find out what is no longer available. Start with the name you would like, then move to any variations you can think of. It may be that you have thought of a new, better name for your weblog since you started it. This is the perfect time to change over, if the domain is available.

Theoretically, .com stands for commercial sites, .net for Web hosts (or ISPs), and .org for nonprofit organizations. That's the protocol, but no one seems to enforce the rules anymore. You may not be able to find a name you like under one of these TLDs, since so many variations are registered already. Many webloggers have turned to alternate TLDs instead. For a while, .nu was quite a fad, and many, many others exist. Go to Joe Clark's Webpage on "alternadomains" for a list of non-U.S. TLDs and information on how to obtain them.

Once you have found an available name, you must register and pay for it. Prices for domain names vary greatly, and more expensive by no means equates with better service. ICANN (The Internet Corporation for Assigned Names and Numbers, the "technical coordination body for the Internet") maintains a list of accredited registrars. Look at the many available registrars and prices. Ask other webloggers where they registered their domain names, and if they experienced any problems with their registrar. If your Web host offers domain registration, look to them first. My Web host offers low-cost domain registration and an easy Web-based interface for managing them.

When buying a domain name, I would advise you to avoid VeriSign (formerly Network Solutions) at all costs. For a long time they were the only available registrar, and, perhaps as a result of the monopoly they held, never seem to have established reliable procedures for managing their customers' data. They are more expensive than many available options and have been known to sell their customers' information to other businesses for "direct marketing campaigns." Though I have never had trouble with them, I have heard so many horror stories regarding the mismanagement of their customers' assets that I now register my domains elsewhere.

Be prepared to pay for your domain with a credit card. It used to be that you had to buy the first two years at once and renew every year thereafter. Currently, some registrars allow you to buy a domain for only one year or even as many as ten. Use your judgment. Whatever term you choose, immediately mark on your calendar the date your renewal will come due. Domain names, especially those ending in .com, .net, and .org, are increasingly hard to come by; if you let your domain lapse, not only will your site one day go dark, but someone else may snatch it up before you can buy it again. This is especially true of .com domains. Unscrupulous individuals set up automated processes for buying any lapsed .com domain—which they then offer to sell for an exorbitant fee to whomever they judge may be interested. If they find the domain to be of little value on the market, they may redirect it to a porn site in order to make a small referral fee for each hit.

As you fill in the necessary information to purchase your domain, follow exactly the instructions given by your Web host for DNS information and the like. Once you have purchased the site, it will take a day or two for it to appear in the database when you do a whois search. In the meantime, upload your files to your new server according to the instructions provided by your host. Try not to check your new URL more than once every few hours. Continue checking at least once a day until your new URL finally brings you to your weblog. Woo-hoo!

Poke around, taking whatever time you need to ensure that your navigational links take you to the proper areas of your entire site. If you want to redesign or to change the architecture of your site in any way, this is the perfect time. Continue to update your old site as usual.

Once you have your new site working to your perfect satisfaction, update your weblog and archives, and redirect visitors from your old site to your new one. Delete your old weblog entries and add one that says:

My weblog has moved. Please visit me at <a href="www.example.org/">www.example.org</a>.

Keep this page up for at least six months to allow infrequent visitors to find your new location.

Once you register a domain, your contact information will be available to whoever looks up your domain using one of the whois services. Since spambots regularly scrape the whois database for email addresses to add to their databases, you *will* experience an increase of spam. You may want to use an alternate email address when registering your domains, but make sure it is one that you check regularly. This is the email address that your registrar will use to contact you when it is time for renewal or to resolve any conflicts about your domain. You may also want to use a P.O. box or business address when you register, since otherwise your home address will be available to anyone who looks at the record for your site.

> Alternadomains
> http://www.fawny.org/alternadomains.html

ISSN Numbers

According to the ISSN website, the ISSN (International Standard Serial Number) is "an eight-digit number which identifies periodical publications as such, including electronic serials." Inspired by Joe Clark, some webloggers have registered their sites as serial publications. I don't know whether anyone has figured out how to leverage this legitimacy to any benefit (press passes, anyone?), but it is kind of fun to think that your site is internationally recognized as a periodical.

> ISSN for weblogs http://www.fawny.org/issn.html

Statistics

You can know exactly what happens on your site, but you can never know for sure who did it, or how many of them there were. Numerous server log analysis tools are available, and each one uses a slightly different method of tracking visitors' movements through your site. Some programs tell you which page most visitors entered through, or which paths through your site they followed. That's very useful if you're running a commercial site, but most webloggers are interested in only a few things: how many people visited my site, which pages did they look at, and where did they come from?

When someone visits your site, it is possible to collect a good deal of information: what operating system their computer uses, which browser, which pages they visit, what page they arrived from, their ISP, and so on. However, it is impossible to know exactly how many people looked at your site. Some people track hits, but a hit is just a request for data; if your weblog contains an HTML file, a graphic header, and a little image to denote permalinks, each page view would require three requests for data (or hits) just to show the page to one person.

Some people track page views, and this may be a crucial measure if you have limited bandwidth available for your account. But keep in mind that one person who visits your site three times in one day will generate the same number of page views as someone who looks at your weblog and then visits your November and December archives—or three people who visit your site one time each. The more times a day you update (especially if your weblog is listed on an update tracker) the further your page view count is likely to deviate from the number of people who visit your site. If you appear on the update trackers each time you post, you probably can increase your page views by updating more frequently, even if your core audience is very small. Page views, like hits, reflect activity on your site.

If you are interested in tracking people rather than activity, the simplest (and I think perfectly satisfactory) way to estimate your audience is to count unique IPs. This figure is generated by counting the number of different IP addresses used by the people who visit your site. Because of the complexities of the network, some individuals will generate more than one IP if they visit your site over a period of time, and many individuals may collectively generate only one. None of the commonly available statistics will give you a completely accurate picture of the size of your audience, but of the measures available, this one correlates most closely to the number of visitors to your site and allows you to reliably track trends.

Free Web hosts rarely provide their users with logs for tracking their visitors. However, there are services that allow you to track your site statistics by embedding a small graphic on your page. Each has its own special formula for calculating visitors and all of them call the various figures by different names. You probably are most interested in tracking the number of visitors who look at your page. Read the documentation to determine which statistic will give you this information. Note that these tracking services may slow down the time it takes for your page to load; if it causes an extreme delay, look for a Web tracking service that is faster.

Most professional Web hosts will provide you with the option to generate server logs for the sites you host with them. They should make available some way to process these logs, though this will be easier or harder depending on the software they run and the documentation they provide. If you wish, you can purchase server log processing software, but some of these packages are very expensive. Once you direct your Web host to collect data about the visitors to your site, you must remember to regularly archive or remove the files from your site. Server logs take up more space than you would imagine, and in only a few months you may find that you have exceeded your disk allotment if you do not remove them.

Acknowledgments

This book is a chance I never thought I would have. It grew out of my weblog and my participation in the ever growing weblog community. I am grateful to all the wonderful professionals at Perseus Publishing who brought this book to life, in particular Leigh Weiner, Jennifer Johnson, Janice Tapia, Alex Camlin, Marvin Martinez, Chrisona Schmidt, Marco Pavia, and especially to David Goehring for taking a chance on me. Special thanks to my editor John Rodzvilla for suggesting me, advocating for me, advising me, and just generally shepherding me through the process of publishing my first book. You have been wonderful.

Thanks to Onda Booker and Linda Stanek for user testing portions of this book. Your efforts truly averted disaster.

Thanks to my mother and father for their absolute belief that I could be anything I wanted to be when I grew up. I also appreciate your patience in waiting for me to decide just what, exactly, that might be. Thanks to my grandmother for demonstrating that adventures can happen at any age. As I make my way through the rest of my life I promise to at least peek through the many doors that open.

This book has benefited immeasurably from the input of my husband, Jesse James Garrett, especially with regard to the sections on journalism and ethics. From our countless hours of discussion about weblogs to your rigorous examination of my many half-formed ideas, this book is smarter and clearer than it ever could have been without you. Thank you for your love, your unwavering belief in me, and your willingness to do the laundry. Your support made this book possible. I now know what it is to have a partner in all things.

Finally, thanks to the weblog community itself. You have educated me, infuriated me, entertained me, and inspired me every day during the last three years. This book is the culmination of everything you have taught me. Thank you for your honesty, your enthusiasm, and above all your generosity in sharing what you know with whomever will listen. What you are doing is new and important. I am privileged to be in your company.

Index

◇ ◇ ◇

This book was set in Dante MT type. Giovanni Mardersteig designed Dante after the Second World War, when printing at the Officinal Bodoni returned to full production. He drew on his experience of using Monotype Bembo and Centaur to design a book face with an italic which worked harmoniously with the roman. Originally hand-cut by Charles Malin, it was adapted for mechanical composition by Monotype in 1957.

◇ ◇ ◇